Reasonable Creatures

REASONABLE CREATURES

Essays on Women and Feminism

KATHA POLLITT

Alfred A. Knopf / *New York* / *1994*

THIS IS A BORZOI BOOK
PUBLISHED BY ALFRED A. KNOPF, INC.

The essays in this collection originally appeared in the following publications.
The Nation: "Contracts and Apple Pie," "Checkbook Maternity," "Fetal Rights," "Hot Flash," "Implants," "Lorena's Army," "Marooned on Gilligan's Island," "Naming and Blaming," "Our Right-to-Lifer," "That Survey," "Who's Afraid of Hillary Clinton? " "Why I Hate Family Values," and "Why We Read"
The New York Times: "Children of Choice," "On the Merits," "The Smurfette Principle," and "Violence in a Man's World"
The New Yorker: "Not Just Bad Sex" and "The Romantic Climacteric"

Library of Congress Cataloging-in-Publication Data
Pollitt, Katha.
Reasonable creatures : essays on women and feminism /
by Katha Pollitt.
p. cm.
ISBN 0-394-57060-X
1. Social problems—Moral and ethical aspects.   2. Social
problems—United States.   3. Feminist ethics—United States.
4. United States—Social conditions—1980–   I. Title.
HN18.P655   1994
305.42'0973—dc20   93-47492
CIP

Manufactured in the United States of America
First Edition

To my father, Basil Riddiford Pollitt,
and to my grandfather, Joseph Levine

Contents

Acknowledgments

I'd like to thank Victor Navasky, editor of *The Nation*, for unfailing encouragement and wobbly deadlines, and JoAnn Wypijewski, *The Nation*'s managing editor, for close readings and tough questions. Thanks also to Nancy Newhouse at *The New York Times*; Adam Gopnik and Deborah Garrison at *The New Yorker*; my editor at Knopf, Victoria Wilson; and my agent, Melanie Jackson.

I'm grateful to many friends for our years-long conversations on the issues discussed in these essays: Anna Fels, Mary Ellen Burns, Katherine Bouton, Ann Snitow, Barbara Ehrenreich, Dierdre English, Deborah Bell, Joshua Freeman, Paul Berman, Randy Cohen, Beth Prince, and Tina Stiefel. And I'm grateful to Paul Mattick, Jr., for reading countless drafts, making countless dinners, and sharing with me his mind and his life.

Introduction

Like Broadway, the novel, and God, feminism has been declared dead many times. Indeed, unlike those other items, it has been declared dead almost from the moment of its birth, by which I mean its birth as a modern political movement in the mid-nineteenth century. Sometimes its demise has been attributed to its success: Yes, yes, women used to be oppressed, but that's all over now. And sometimes its demise has been attributed to its irrelevance: Women don't *want* to be liberated, as Marilyn Quayle famously put it at the 1992 Republican convention, from their "essential nature" as stay-at-home wives and mothers. (It did not seem to occur to Ms. Quayle that homemakers might not be flattered to have their way of life presented as biological fate rather than a free choice—much less that such women, like their wage-earning sisters, might have something to gain from reproductive rights, an end to sexual violence and economic discrimination, and husbands who washed the dishes without being asked.)

I began writing about so-called women's issues during the 1980s, a decade that was widely portrayed in the media as one long funeral for feminism. But what a difference a few years and a Senate hearing or two can make: Today, feminist issues—from sexual harassment to lesbian motherhood to equal representation in government—are once again big news. When fashion magazines start wondering if maybe women shouldn't just forget about losing that last five pounds, you *know* American women have turned some sort of corner.

It was bound to happen. During the Reagan and Bush years, the media worked overtime portraying women as divided against each other in every conceivable way: promiscuous versus chaste, single versus married, pro-choice versus pro-life, mothers versus childless women, mothers in the paid labor force versus those in the home and, of course, "feminists" (a strange amalgam of upper-middle-class white professionals, Goddess worshippers, lesbian karate experts and hairy-legged antiporn crusaders) versus the vast majority of American women. Meanwhile, however, back in the real world, more and more women were finding themselves shuttling back and forth between these supposedly rigid categories. Most women work *and* have children; marry, but maybe not for long. The student who has an abortion at nineteen becomes the secretary who has a baby at twenty-six. Women who feel demeaned by men's interest in pornography have forced supermarket romances to feature nonvirginal heroines and semi-explicit sex scenes, own vibrators and know how to use them and roll their eyes at Hollywood scripts that suggest that a woman married to a man who looks like Woody Harrelson would hesitate to sleep with one who looks like Robert Redford, even for a million dollars. Women even want to have sexual experiences and not be raped or abused—although as the controversy over campus date rape shows, this particular concept seems strangely difficult for many, including some women, to grasp.

A recent *Time* cover story ("Are MEN Really That Bad?") endorses Camille Paglia's view that women who wish to avoid assault should not drink on dates or visit men in their rooms. Why not advise *men* not to drink on dates, and remind them that sex with a willing and enthusiastic partner is more fun, not to mention more legal, than wrestling a frightened, resentful and semi-stupefied woman into acquiescence?

For many people, feminism is one of those words of which, as St. Augustine said about time, they know the meaning as long as no one is asking. In the popular stereotype, a feminist is a woman who wants power over men or to do without men or to be like a man. In the view of Carol Gilligan and other "difference feminists," it is to reclaim and celebrate the supposedly feminine virtues of caring, connection, altruism and cooperation. And in the view of innumerable popularizers, feminism is a kind of assertiveness training, by which women can overcome external barriers to professional success.

For me, to be a feminist is to answer the question "Are women human?" with a yes. It is not about whether women are better than, worse than or identical with men. And it's certainly not about trading personal liberty—abortion, divorce, sexual self-expression—for social protection as wives and mothers, as pro-life feminists propose. It's about justice, fairness and access to the broad range of human experience. It's about women consulting their own well-being and being judged as individuals rather than as members of a class with one personality, one social function, one road to happiness. It's about women having intrinsic value as persons rather than contingent value as a means to an end for others: fetuses, children, "the family," men.

It says a great deal about our society that this idea is so unsettling to so many, and that the social measures that would forward it—reproductive freedom, including easy access to abortion; an end to job and pay discrimination; paid parental leave, day care and so forth—have been so bitterly resisted. Sometimes it seems as though government, the media and business are just holding their breath, hoping that the 1950s will come back, like Halley's comet. What's interesting, though, is that despite the backlash and twelve years of Republican administrations explicitly hostile to women's rights, the eighties were not the fifties. But then, the fifties weren't the fifties either, except on television. It seems pretty clear that no matter how often women are told they're secretly miserable, and no matter how hard the dominant culture works to make them openly miserable, women are not going to go back home for good. Sooner or later, social institutions will have to accommodate this fact, and so will men.

The essays collected here were written in response to various events and ideas—news stories like the Baby M case and the Palm Beach rape trial; political developments like the growing prominence of the pro-life movement and the rise of "family values" as a social-policy panacea; debates like those over "fetal rights," battered women and date rape. I like to think that they are drawn together by a common concern for women's entitlement to full human rights: to say what happens to their own bodies, to develop their abilities without being defined and constrained by stereotypes of the "feminine," to make their own choices and their own mistakes without being punished for them more than a man would be. I've taken my title from Mary Wollstonecraft, the first woman to present a full-dress argument for female equality. "I wish to see women neither heroines nor brutes," she wrote in *A Vindication of the Rights of Women*, "but reasonable creatures."

Human beings, in other words. No more, no less.

Reasonable Creatures

That Survey:
Being Wedded Is Not Always Bliss

I n a less conservative era, an academic study projecting a modest decline in the percentage of college-educated white women who marry might have sparked a round of journalistic applause: "Good News About Marriage: Finally Women Can Afford to Wait for Mr. Right," for instance, or "Despite Heavy Pressure From Pop Psychologists, Women Still Say No to Men Who Chew with Mouth Open." In fact, in a less conservative era "Marriage Patterns in the United States," by David Bloom, Neil Bennett and Patricia Craig, might not have got much media attention at all, but that, to put it mildly, is not the sort of era we are living in.

What really appeared on the cover of *Newsweek* was a graph showing that as single women grow older their "chances" of marrying descend as precipitously as the tracks of the Man Who Skied Down Mount Everest. "Are These OLD MAIDS?" demanded *People* over photographs of Diane Sawyer, Sharon Gless, Donna Mills and Linda Ronstadt. "A

Harvard-Yale Study Says That Most Single Women Over 35 Can Forget About Marriage." To a steady funereal drumbeat, a parade of contrite professional women has been marched across the national consciousness:

"I think I was twenty-two until I was thirty-eight."

"Men have become an obsession with me."

"I feel like my mother's finger is wagging at me, telling me I shouldn't have waited."

Actual women have allowed themselves to be quoted saying those things. Talk about letting down the side.

Of course, not all single women are weeping into their newly purchased copies of *Smart Women, Foolish Choices*. Many are simply furious. "The study reinforces the view that women over thirty are desperate and powerless in their relationships with men. Ours not to choose but only—hope, hope—to be chosen," said one outraged friend of mine. "It's a real put-down," said another. "It's saying, You wanted independence? Well, you got it, and the joke's on you." That is indeed the message the media are using the study to convey. But is that what the study says? Are its findings so dire?

Basically the study plots the relation between two facts: One, during the postwar baby boom each year's crop of new-borns was larger than the one before; and two, women tend to marry "up"—men two or three years older than themselves and at least as well educated—while men tend to marry "down." Thus, a woman born in 1955 is looking for her mate in the smaller pool of men born in 1953. There aren't enough of them to go around to start with, and the longer she waits, the fewer there are. By thirty, a white college-educated woman's likelihood of marrying—that is, marrying up—is one in five; by thirty-five, it's one in twenty. And the situation for black women is even worse.

The "man shortage" is thus really an "older-man shortage," and a temporary one at that, given that after the baby boom each year brought fewer births than the year before, so a woman born in 1965, say, can have her pick of older men, if that's what she wants. But why assume that today's thirty-five-year-old woman will scorn today's thirty-three-year-old man? Good question. In fact, the number of marriages between older women and younger men is on the increase. There are other problems with the study as well. As the researchers keep telling reporters, their findings are based entirely on census data. For reasons best known to themselves, they interviewed no college-educated single women, and thus have no idea how many want to marry, think they want to marry but only fall in love with Greek sponge divers, are contentedly cohabiting in nonmarital bliss, are gay, hate the very thought of marriage or just don't care one way or the other.

The study is just what its authors say it is: an exercise in demographics, not desire—and rather old-fashioned demographics at that, for it recognizes only two categories of women, single and married. Thus, for statistical purposes I count as a single even though I've been living monogamously with a man for six years, only one year short of the duration of the average American marriage. And I am far from alone; as marriage rates have declined, live-together rates have soared. On a societal level, that means that "single" and "married" are no longer such useful classifications. On a personal level it means that would-be-married baby boomers can take heart: When live-togethers, lesbians and alone-by-choicers are removed from the statistical pool of singles, the prospects brighten considerably for those who remain. So far, only *Mademoiselle* and *Self* have pointed out this rather obvious bit of math. No wonder the researchers keep insisting that their findings are being blown way out of proportion.

So why the fuss? The study projects, after all, that eight out of ten white college-educated women will marry. Since in past generations nine out of ten did so, what we are talking about here is a decline that virtually disappears when one factors in the voluntarily unmarried. That is surely a flimsy basis on which to urge sensible adult women to beat their breasts for having spurned a blind date with Aunt Hilda's best friend's son's college roommate fifteen years ago, or for being so romantic or so practical or so ambitious or so frivolous or so—feminist? Could that be the word we are looking for?

Here is another set of statistics. Married women earn $626 a week for every $1,000 earned by men; single women who work full time earn $910. Wives describe themselves as less happy than do married men or single women (only single men are more dissatisfied), and they are much more likely than single women to be clinically depressed. As many as one in seven women have been raped by their husbands; one in four have been beaten at least once. Despite the tremendous influx of married women into the workforce, men do only 6 percent more housework than they did twenty years ago, and the husbands of women who work outside the home pitch in only slightly more than the husbands of housewives. All of which helps to explain why, according to a *Woman's Day* survey, only 50 percent of wives say they would marry their husbands again.

And here is another set. A woman marrying today has a dead even chance of finding herself in divorce court, where, as study after study has documented, the system tends to shortchange wives. Although both the domestic demands of marriage and its implied promise of lifelong security encourage a woman to put her career on hold, only 15 percent of divorcing women are awarded alimony or rehabilitative (interesting word) maintenance. The average allotment in New York State is $4,000 a year. Nationally, the average court-awarded child-support payment is $34 a week—a ludicrous sum, but only half of ex-husbands bother to pay it in full. Perhaps most alarming, although women are overwhelmingly their children's primary caregivers, a man who pursues a custody suit has an even chance of winning. The fact that he works proves he is a stable citizen and good father, while a mother is caught in a double bind: If she works, she's neglectful; if she doesn't, she's a parasite.

This, then, is the institution to which today's single professional women are being urged to flock for happiness and fulfillment. Is it any wonder they're taking their time?

Viewed against this background of dismal facts, the study looks positively cheerful. What it reveals is not that women are too busy plotting corporate takeovers to pencil "get married" into their Filofaxes (for all the hoopla about female yuppies, as of 1982, only 1.4 percent of white female managers earned $50,000 or more, and the percentage of nonwhite female managers earning that amount was too small to measure). It's that for the first time in history large numbers of women have enough economic independence to look very closely at the candidates for their hand, and the kind of marriage they are offering. The stereotype of prosperous but desperate thirty-five-year-olds could not be more wrong: Desperate is knowing that you have to marry and stay married to survive.

So, you are probably asking, if the study contains only no news or good news, who's buying all those copies of *How to Get Married in 90 Days?* Is not the most obvious fact of social life in New York the enormous number of intelligent, pleasant, attractive single women who would like to have a serious relationship but haven't had a date since New Year's Eve, 1983? As so often where women are concerned, the good news is also the bad news. It is indeed cause for rejoicing that large numbers of women can reject the traditional hierarchical marriage, in which women barter domestic service and emotional submission for economic support and social recognition, and can hold out for a marriage that promises intimacy and equality. But that doesn't mean that those women will find one.

Then again, it never did. Perhaps the most striking aspect of the brouhaha surrounding the study is that it is universally regarded as describing a bizarre new development. In fact, for at least a hundred years there have been more educated, independent women than there were men who wanted to marry them. The silk-bloused single professional of the 1980s is the great-granddaughter of the bicycle-skirted New Woman of the 1880s and 1890s, who horrified pundits and fascinated novelists from H. G. Wells to Henry James. Then as now, the blame for her unmarried state was divided between demographics, which made millions of women "superfluous," and feminism, which spoiled them for the "sacrifice" of marriage. Thus, the most important thing to note about today's single professional is that a hundred years ago—or fifty years ago— she would very likely have been unmarried, too. It's just that there are more of her now, and unlike the New Woman, she has a sex life, which upsets a lot of people.

It's comforting, perhaps, to see oneself as part of a historical tradition instead of as a mere statistical bulge. The deeper implications, however, are disturbing. America, after all, has had a full century to get used to the idea of egalitarian marriage and all those other daring Gay Nineties notions. But if the study tells us that women are no longer dependent on marriage for sex or a home or a set of nice dishes, it also tells us that men still want wives who will put husbands first, and that marriage as an institution still favors that desire. Public policy, which could help defuse this conflict, reinforces it. The United States has no national day-care system, and is virtually alone among Western industrialized nations in having no legally mandated maternity leave—let alone paternity leave or sick-child leave. We don't even have public nursery schools. The culture of professional work, too, is structured according to the traditional male life pattern. If careers tacitly assume a support system in the form of a stay-at-home spouse, too bad for women. If the twenties and thirties, when professionals are scrambling their hardest, happen to be women's prime reproductive years, too bad again.

In a society committed to sexual equality, single professional women would be applauded as pioneers. They are breaking down all sorts of ancient prejudices, from the sexual double standard to the connection between femininity and submissiveness, poverty, dependence, powerlessness and incompetence. In the current climate of antifeminist backlash, however, they are loose cannons on the deck. Clearly, the hope in many quarters is that they will give up this careers nonsense if it is made sufficiently arduous, and get back under male "protection" where they belong—even though that protection, in terms of a guarantee of lifelong support, no longer exists.

This is the underlying message of a variety of seemingly disparate contributions to the public discourse. While Sylvia Ann Hewlett, in *A Lesser Life*, blames the women's movement for the absence of social supports for working mothers, as though the feminist goal of shared parenting were a piece of utopian lunacy, Deborah Fallows, in *A Mother's Work*, portrays women who use day care as shallow materialists, as though stay-at-home moms could waltz back into the workplace whenever they wished. While the Reagan Administration does its best to scuttle affirmative action and thwart comparable worth for pink-collar women, their white-collar sisters find themselves mysteriously "topping out," hitting the "glass ceiling" of covert discrimination. Abortion is under attack. Nonmarital sex is under attack. Infertile women are selfish for having put careers before pregnancy, as though no man ever insisted on postponing fatherhood; but women who beat the clock by having babies without husbands are selfish, too.

Who would have thought that the modest demands of women for decent jobs, equal access to education, shared domestic responsibilities and all the rest would evoke such a torrent of censure? But then who would have thought that in 1986 women would have fewer methods of contraception to choose from than they had ten years ago?

The media coverage of the study, if not quite the study itself, is just another crack of the backlash. Women can't "have it all." Women must "choose": a career or a husband. By focusing on demographics, which cannot be changed and are no one's fault, commentators avoid asking hard questions about the social context that gives the demographics whatever limited significance they have—questions about the structure of work and marriage and childrearing and society, and about the ways in which those work together to confront both single and married women with a dazzling array of Catch-22s.

Questions about—what a thought—men. It is curious that the study offers no figures on men. Ostensibly, that is because of the "poor quality" of the data, and perhaps that really is the reason. By its silence, however, the study appears to confirm the all too popular assumption that a college-educated heterosexual man's "chance" of marrying is a solid 100 percent right into the grave. Demographically, maybe so, but marriage does, after all, take two. Why assume that baby boom bachelors are God's gift to single women rather than those women's rejects, the men least able to deal with women's raised expectations of marriage?

If our magazine moralists applied themselves to those issues, they might discover that what keeps today's college-educated women unmarried isn't numbers. It's sexism.

1986

Children of Choice

There were a lot of kids at our housewarming party—babies, toddlers, even one or two who were big enough to pointedly inform their parents how bored they were. The last time we moved, seven years ago, there hadn't been any. So here we are, I thought, almost forty, and really it hasn't turned out so badly for a lot of the women I know: We've got nice husbands—maybe not the first man we married, but everyone makes mistakes—work that interests us and (except for the writers among us) pays a grown-up living, and adorable, healthy children we love to bits.

I don't mean to say that our numbers have all turned up in the Grand Happiness Lottery—who knows what even your best friend is thinking at four in the morning?—but no one's drinking or drugging or sunk in a sour mist of frustration and rage, and no one's sanity is fraying around the edges, as happened to some of the women on the block where I grew up. There's another thing we have in common: No one had a baby before she was ready, wild to be a mother. And birth control being what it is, that means that many of the women in our living room that day had had abortions.

It's a measure of the changing national climate where abortion is concerned that I feel uneasy about writing this for publication. The so-called right-to-lifers have not yet scored a direct hit against abortion, unless you count clinic bombings, which I do. But they've done something that may in the long run have an even more serious effect: They've set the terms of the debate. Have you noticed? It's not about women's bodies anymore, or family planning, or sexual freedom. It's about women's "convenience," to use the pro-life buzzword, versus babies' lives. Framed like that, the abortion debate can turn out only one way. If the fetus is a person, how can its life be less important than a woman's liberty and pursuit of happiness?

Faced with the tremendously emotion-laden image of the vulnerable, innocent preborn baby, defenders of legal abortion tend to respond with another set of emotional images: pregnant schoolgirls, rape and incest victims, those who die in pregnancy or childbirth or give birth to infants with horrendous, fatal conditions like Tay-Sachs disease or AIDS. The images are real, all right—I know a woman who got pregnant from a date rape, and another with a heart condition that could have killed her had she been forced to carry a child to term. But look how much ground they concede. What if it's not your life that's at stake but "just" your health? Or your diploma? Or your job? Or your marriage? What if you weren't forced to have sex, and you're not fifteen but twenty-five—or thirty-five?

By constantly placing abortion in a context of extreme situations—sexual crime, maternal deaths, doomed babies—one labels it an extreme response. And that sets the stage for someone—George Bush, for example—to propose a "compromise": permit abortion for limited classes of "hard cases" and forbid it for everyone else. But unwanted pregnancies are the stuff of everyday.

Here are some reasons why women I know became pregnant: because her IUD came out one morning; because her husband failed—once, in thirteen years!—to put on his condom in time; because she and her live-in trusted to the calendar and had a diaphragmless tryst on the beach; because she thought breast-feeding prevented ovulation and, anyway, she'd given birth just six weeks before. Stupid, trivial reasons, the same sort of reasons you might give for missing a train. (I'm sorry, you apologize, I misread the schedule, I couldn't find a taxi, the meeting ran late.)

Most of the time, people catch their trains, and most of the time, adult, middle-class, sensible women take care of birth control, and birth control takes care of them. (I'm not talking about teenagers or the poor or the helpless here.) But a woman has about thirty years of potentially fertile sex—that's a long time to go without a slip-up. That's one reason why more than half the pregnancies in this country are accidents, and why, if you follow a hundred women over their reproductive lives, forty-six of them will have had an abortion by menopause, and many will have had more than one.

The abortion rate is always discussed in terms of values, to use the current cliché. Are Americans (by which is really meant American women) too promiscuous, too selfish, too frivolous, too in love with control? But surely we are not more so than the Swedes, those fabled hedonists, or less so than the tradition-bound Greeks. Why, then, do Swedish women have fewer abortions than American women, and Greek women more than twice as many?

All over the industrialized West, women want education and jobs, couples want small, planned families, and people— men and women, married and unmarried—want sexual intimacy. A society's abortion rate is a measure of its failure to meet these imperatives straightforwardly: by making it easy to get contraception that works, by demystifying sex, by making children the responsibility of all.

Moralists, including some who are pro-choice, like to say that abortion isn't or shouldn't be a method of birth control. But that's just what abortion is—a bloody, clumsy method of birth control. Those who find abortion immoral have a duty to come forward with other solutions to the unwanted-pregnancy problem. But where are the pro-life voices shouting for increased funding for contraceptive research, sex education and true universal access to family planning? It is the movement's lack of enthusiasm for a birth-control crusade—even the non-Catholics don't campaign for contraception in a way you'd notice—that reveals the pro-life cause as more about shoring up Victorian sexual values than about stopping abortion.

Here are some reasons why friends of mine had abortions: They were in college and wanted to graduate. They were in graduate school or professional training and wanted to finish. They could not care for a child and keep their jobs. They were not in a relationship that could sustain parenthood at that time. They were not, in short, ready or able to be good mothers yet, although those who have children are good mothers now. Hard-hearted calculations of "convenience"? Only if you think that pregnancy is the price of sex, that women have no work but motherhood, and that children don't need grown-up parents.

The fact is, when your back is against the wall of unwanted pregnancy, it doesn't matter whether or not you think the fetus is a person. That's why, in this country, Roman Catholic women, who are less likely to use effective birth control, have a higher abortion rate than Jews or Protestants. Women do what they need to do in order to lead reasonable lives, and they always have. Nowadays, a reasonable life does not include shotgun weddings, or dropping out of school, or embracing the minimum wage for life. Still less does it include bearing a baby for strangers to adopt, as George Bush blithely suggests.

My friends who had abortions believed that having a baby at that time of their lives would be a disaster. Not an inconvenience, a disaster. Five, ten and fifteen years later, not one of them regrets her choice, just as not one of them regrets her decision, five or three or two years ago, to become a mother.

Looking around my living room, I didn't see a problem with that. And I still don't.

1988

Why We Read:
Canon to the Right of Me . . .

For the past couple of years we've all been witness to a furious debate about the literary canon. What books should be assigned to students? What books should critics discuss? What books should the rest of us read, and who are "we" anyway? Like everyone else, I've given these questions some thought, and when an invitation came my way, I leaped to produce my own manifesto. But to my surprise, when I sat down to write—in order to discover, as E. M. Forster once said, what I really think—I found that I agreed with all sides in the debate at once.

Take the conservatives. Now, this rather dour collection of scholars and diatribists—Allan Bloom, Hilton Kramer, John Silber and so on—are not a particularly appealing group of people. They are arrogant, they are rude, they are gloomy, they do not suffer fools gladly, and everywhere they look, fools are what they see. All good reasons not to elect them to public office, as Massachusetts voters decided when they rejected Silber's 1990 gubernatorial bid. But what is so terrible, really, about what they are saying? I, too, believe that some books are more profound, more complex, more essential to an understanding of our culture than others; I, too, am appalled to think of students graduating from college not having read Homer, Plato, Virgil, Milton, Tolstoy—all writers, dead white Western men though they be, whose works have meant a great deal to me. As a teacher of literature and of writing, I too have seen at first hand how ill-educated many students are, and how little aware they are of this important fact about themselves. Last year I taught a graduate seminar in the writing of poetry. None of my students had read more than a smattering of poems by anyone, male or female, published more than ten years ago. Robert Lowell was as far outside their frame of reference as Alexander Pope. When I gently suggested to one student that it might benefit her to read some poetry if she planned to spend her life writing it, she told me that yes, she knew she should read more but when she encountered a really good poem it only made her depressed. That contemporary writing has a history which it profits us to know in some depth, that we ourselves were not born yesterday, seems too obvious even to argue.

But ah, say the liberals, the canon exalted by the conservatives is itself an artifact of history. Sure, some books are more rewarding than others, but why can't we change our minds about which books those are? The canon itself was not always as we know it today: Until the 1920s, *Moby-Dick* was shelved with the boys' adventure stories. If T. S. Eliot could single-handedly dethrone the Romantic poets in favor of the neglected Metaphysicals and place John Webster alongside Shakespeare, why can't we dip into the sea of stories and fish out Edith Wharton or Virginia Woolf? And this position, too, makes a great deal of sense to me. After all, alongside the many good reasons for a book to end up on the required-reading shelf are some rather suspect reasons for its exclusion: because it was written by a woman and therefore presumed to be too slight; because it was written by a black person and therefore presumed to be too unsophisticated or to reflect too special a case. By all means, say the liberals, let's have great books and a shared culture. But let's make sure that all the different kinds of greatness are represented and that the culture we share reflects the true range of human experience.

If we leave the broadening of the canon up to the conservatives, this will never happen, because to them change only means defeat. Look at the recent fuss over the latest edition of the Great Books series published by Encyclopedia Britannica, headed by that old snake-oil salesman Mortimer Adler. Four women have now been added to the series: Virginia Woolf, Willa Cather, Jane Austen and George Eliot. That's nice, I suppose, but really! Jane Austen has been a certified Great Writer for a hundred years! Lionel Trilling said so! There's something truly absurd about the conservatives earnestly sitting in judgment on the illustrious dead, as though up in Writers' Heaven Jane and George and Willa and Virginia were breathlessly waiting to hear if they'd finally made it into the club, while Henry Fielding, newly dropped from the list, howls in outer darkness and the Brontës, presumably, stamp their feet in frustration and hope for better luck in twenty years, when *Jane Eyre* and *Wuthering Heights* will suddenly turn out to have qualities of greatness never before detected in their pages. It's like Poets' Corner at Manhattan's Cathedral of St. John the Divine, where mortal men—and a woman or two—of letters actually vote on which immortals to honor with a plaque, a process no doubt complete with electoral campaigns, compromise candidates and all the rest of the underside of the literary life. "No, I'm sorry, I just can't vote for Whitman. I'm a Washington Irving man myself."

Well, a liberal is not a very exciting thing to be, and so

we have the radicals, who attack the concepts of "greatness," "shared," "culture" and "lists." (I'm overlooking here the ultraradicals, who attack the "privileging" of "texts," as they insist on calling books, and think one might as well spend one's college years deconstructing "Leave It to Beaver.") Who is to say, ask the radicals, what is a great book? What's so terrific about complexity, ambiguity, historical centrality and high seriousness? If *The Color Purple*, say, gets students thinking about their own experience, maybe they ought to read it and forget about ———, and here you can fill in the name of whatever classic work you yourself found dry and tedious and never got around to finishing. For the radicals the notion of a shared culture is a lie, because it means presenting as universally meaningful and politically neutral books that reflect the interests and experiences and values of privileged white men at the expense of those of others—women, blacks, Latinos, Asians, the working class, whomever. Why not scrap the one-list-for-everyone idea and let people connect with books that are written by people like themselves about people like themselves? It will be a more accurate reflection of a multifaceted and conflict-ridden society, and will do wonders for everyone's self-esteem, except, of course, living white men—but they have too much self-esteem already.

Now, I have to say that I dislike the radicals' vision intensely. How foolish to argue that Chekhov has nothing to say to a black woman—or, for that matter, to me—merely because he is Russian, long dead, a man. The notion that one reads to increase one's self-esteem sounds to me like more snake oil. Literature is not an aerobics class or a session at the therapist's. But then I think of myself as a child, leafing through anthologies of poetry for the names of women. I never would have admitted that I needed a role model, even if that awful term had existed back in the prehistory of which I speak, but why was I so excited to find a female name, even when, as was often the case, it was attached to a poem of no interest to me whatsoever? Anna Laetitia Barbauld, author of "Life! I know not what thou art/But know that thou and I must part!"; Lady Anne Lindsay, writer of plaintive ballads in incomprehensible Scots dialect, and the other minor female poets included by chivalrous Sir Arthur Quiller-Couch in the old *Oxford Book of English Verse*: I have to admit it, just by their presence in that august volume they did something for me. And although it had not much to do with reading or writing, it was an important thing they did.

Now, what are we to make of this spluttering debate, in which charges of imperialism are met by equally passionate accusations of vandalism, in which each side hates the others, and yet each one seems to have its share of reason? Perhaps what we have here is one of those debates in which the opposing sides, unbeknownst to themselves, share a myopia that will turn out to be the most telling feature of the whole discussion: a debate, for instance, like that of our Founding Fathers over the nature of the franchise. Think of all the energy and passion spent pondering the question of property qualifications or direct versus legislative elections, while all along, unmentioned and unimagined, was the fact—to us so central—that women, not to mention slaves, were never considered for any kind of vote.

Something is being overlooked: the state of reading, and books, and literature in our country at this time. Why, ask yourself, is everyone so hot under the collar about what to put on the required-reading shelf? It is because while we have been arguing so fiercely about which books make the best medicine, the patient has been slipping deeper and deeper into a coma.

Let us imagine a country in which reading is a popular voluntary activity. There, parents read books for their own edification and pleasure, and are seen by their children at this silent and mysterious pastime. These parents also read to their children, give them books for presents, talk to them about books and underwrite, with their taxes, a public library system that is open all day, every day. In school—where an attractive library is invariably to be found—the children study certain books together but also have an active reading life of their own. Years later it may even be hard for them to remember if they read *Jane Eyre* at home and Judy Blume in class, or the other way around. In college young people continue to be assigned certain books, but far more important are the books they discover for themselves, browsing in the library, in bookstores, on the shelves of friends, one book leading to another, back and forth in history and across languages and cultures. After graduation they continue to read, and in the fullness of time produce a new generation of readers. Oh, happy land! I wish we all lived there.

In that other country of real readers—voluntary, active, self-determined readers—a debate like the current one over the canon would not be taking place. Or if it did, it would be as a kind of parlor game: What books would *you* take to a desert island? Everyone would know that the top-ten list was merely a tiny fraction of the books one would read in a lifetime. It would not seem racist or sexist or hopelessly hidebound to put Hawthorne on the syllabus and not Toni Morrison. It would be more like putting oatmeal and not noodles on the breakfast menu—a choice part arbitrary, part a nod to the national past, part, dare one say it, a kind of reverse affirmative action: School might frankly be the place where one read the books that are a little off-putting, that have gone a little cold, that you might pass over because they do not address, in reader-friendly contemporary fashion, the issues most immediately at stake in modern life, but that, with a little study, turn out to have a great deal to say. Being on the list wouldn't mean so much. It might even add to a writer's cachet *not* to be on the list, to be in one way or another too heady, too daring, too exciting to be ground up into institutional fodder for teenagers. Generations of high school students have been spoiled for George Eliot by being forced to read *Silas Marner* at a tender age. One can imagine a whole new readership for her if grown-ups were left to approach *Middlemarch* and *Daniel Deronda* with open minds, at their leisure.

Of course, they rarely do. In America today the assumption underlying the canon debate is that the books on the list are the only books that are going to be read, and if the list is dropped no books are going to be read. Becoming a textbook is a book's only chance; all sides take that for granted. And so all agree not to mention certain things that they themselves, as highly educated people and, one assumes, devoted readers, know perfectly well. For example, that if you read only twenty-five, or fifty, or a hundred books, you can't understand them, however well chosen they are. And that if you don't have an independent reading life—and very few students do —you won't *like* reading the books on the list and will forget them the minute you finish them. And that books have, or should have, lives beyond the syllabus—thus, the totally misguided attempt to put current literature in the classroom. How strange to think that people need professorial help to read John Updike or Alice Walker, writers people actually do read for fun. But all sides agree: If it isn't taught, it doesn't count.

Let's look at the canon question from another angle. Instead of asking what books we want others to read, let's ask why we read books ourselves. I think the canon debaters are being a little disingenuous here, are suppressing, in the interest of their own agendas, their personal experience of reading. Sure, we read to understand our American culture and history, and we also read to recover neglected masterpieces, and to learn more about the accomplishments of our subgroup and thereby, as I've admitted about myself, increase our self-esteem. But what about reading for the aesthetic pleasures of language, form, image? What about reading to learn something new, to have a vicarious adventure, to follow the workings of an interesting, if possibly skewed, narrow and ill-tempered mind? What about reading for the story? For an expanded sense of sheer human variety? There are a thousand reasons why a book might have a claim on our time and attention other than its canonization. I once infuriated an acquaintance by asserting that Trollope, although in many ways a lesser writer than Dickens, possessed some wonderful qualities Dickens lacked: a more realistic view of women, a more skeptical view of good intentions, a subtler sense of humor, a drier vision of life which I myself found congenial. You'd think I'd advocated throwing Dickens out and replacing him with a toaster. Because Dickens is a certified Great Writer, and Trollope is not.

Am I saying anything different from what Randall Jarrell said in his great 1953 essay "The Age of Criticism"? Not really, so I'll quote him. Speaking of the literary gatherings of the era, Jarrell wrote:

> If, at such parties, you wanted to talk about *Ulysses* or *The Castle* or *The Brothers Karamazov* or *The Great Gatsby* or Graham Greene's last novel—Important books—you were at the right place. (Though you weren't so well off if you wanted to talk about *Remembrance of Things Past*. Important, but too long.) But if you wanted to talk about Turgenev's novelettes, or *The House of the Dead*, or *Lavengro*, or *Life on the Mississippi*, or *The Old Wives' Tale*, or *The Golovlyov Family*, or Cunningham-Grahame's stories, or Saint-Simon's memoirs, or *Lost Illusions*, or *The Beggar's Opera*, or *Eugen Onegin*, or *Little Dorrit*, or the *Burnt Njal Saga*, or *Persuasion*, or *The Inspector-General*, or *Oblomov*, or *Peer Gynt*, or *Far from the Madding Crowd*, or *Out of Africa*, or the *Parallel Lives*, or *A*

Dreary Story, or *Debits and Credits*, or *Arabia Deserta*, or *Elective Affinities*, or *Schweik*, or—any of a thousand good or interesting but Unimportant books, you couldn't expect a very ready knowledge or sympathy from most of the readers there. They had looked at the big sights, the current sights, hard, with guides and glasses; and those walks in the country, over unfrequented or thrice-familiar territory, all alone— those walks from which most of the joy and good of reading come—were walks that they hadn't gone on very often.

I suspect that most canon debaters have taken those solitary rambles, if only out of boredom—how many times, after all, can you reread the *Aeneid*, or *Mrs. Dalloway*, or *Cotton Comes to Harlem* (to pick one book from each column)? But those walks don't count, because of another assumption all sides hold in common, which is that the purpose of reading is none of the many varied and delicious satisfactions I've mentioned; it's medicinal. The chief end of reading is to produce a desirable kind of person and a desirable kind of society. A respectful, high-minded citizen of a unified society for the conservatives, an up-to-date and flexible sort for the liberals, a subgroup-identified, robustly confident one for the radicals. How pragmatic, how moralistic, how American! The culture debaters turn out to share a secret suspicion of culture itself, as well as the antipornographer's belief that there is a simple, one-to-one correlation between books and behavior. Read the conservatives' list and produce a nation of sexists and racists —or a nation of philosopher kings. Read the liberals' list and produce a nation of spineless relativists—or a nation of open-minded world citizens. Read the radicals' list and produce a nation of psychobabblers and ancestor-worshippers—or a nation of stalwart proud-to-be-me pluralists.

But is there any list of a few dozen books that can have such a magical effect, for good or for ill? Of course not. It's like arguing that a perfectly nutritional breakfast cereal is enough food for the whole day. And so the canon debate is really an argument about what books to cram down the resistant throats of a resentful captive populace of students; and the trick is never to mention the fact that, in such circumstances, one book is as good, or as bad, as another. Because, as the debaters know from their own experience as readers, books are not pills that produce health when ingested in measured doses. Books do not shape character in any simple way—if, indeed, they do so at all—or the most literate would be the most virtuous instead of just the ordinary run of humanity with larger vocabularies. Books cannot mold a common national purpose when, in fact, people are honestly divided about what kind of country they want—and are divided, moreover, for very good and practical reasons, as they always have been.

For these burly and strenuous purposes, books are all but useless. The way books affect us is an altogether more subtle, delicate, wayward and individual, not to say private, affair. And that reading is being made to bear such an inappropriate and simplistic burden speaks to the poverty both of culture and of frank political discussion in our time.

On his deathbed, Dr. Johnson—once canonical, now more admired than read—is supposed to have said to a friend who was energetically rearranging his bedclothes, "Thank you, this will do all that a pillow can do." One might say that the canon debaters are all asking of their handful of chosen books that it do a great deal more than any handful of books can do.

1991

Violence in a Man's World

We were talking in the playground, another mother and I, about Lisa Bianco. She, you may remember, was the battered Indiana woman who finally, after hundreds of attacks, succeeded in having her ex-husband put in prison, only to be murdered by him on a brief furlough.

"What did she expect?" my fellow mom said angrily. "There's only so much the system can do. She should have gotten a gun and blasted him."

As it happens, a gun would not have helped Ms. Bianco much, unless she was willing to spend the rest of her life sitting in the living room, loaded for bear. She believed, after all, that her attacker was safely locked up at last, and had repeatedly begged the authorities to inform her if he ever got out of prison. Just the week before, a note to that effect had been placed in his file—where it was promptly ignored.

The interesting thing about my playground acquaintance coming up with this gun idea, though, is not its impracticality.

It's that she is a government lawyer. And if she can't come up with a better way to protect the Lisa Biancos of America than for them to do it themselves, we're *really* in trouble.

But then, so we are. Lisa Bianco was only the most recent in a rash of similar stories (three this winter on Long Island alone) in which battered women followed all the rules—reported the assaults, hired lawyers, got orders of protection, kept in touch with the police—and were murdered for their pains. Not a strong argument for working within the system, but women who follow my friend's advice and defend themselves are likely to find the system wakes up with a vengeance.

Remember Karen Straw from Queens? Having pleaded in vain for protection against her violent estranged husband, she stabbed him after he raped her in front of her children, and found herself on trial for murder. Her case attracted a lot of attention and she was acquitted—but our prisons are full of battered women who didn't have Karen Straw's luck, if you can call it that.

Think of Diane Pikul, killed by her stock-analyst husband when she asked for a divorce. Jennifer Levin and Kathleen Holland, strangled by boyfriends who claimed it was all part of "rough sex." Thirteen-year-old Kelly Tinyes, slain by a neighbor. Theresa Saldana, the actress, whose slasher is scheduled for early release from prison despite his many threats against her life. Think of the unnamed women in the headlines not so long ago—two gang-raped and thrown from rooftops, the jogger in Central Park. Think of all the women who have not entered the folklore of crime because their beatings and/or rapes and/or murders lacked the appropriate ingredients for full-dress media treatment—which include, alas, being white, young, middle-class and, as the tabloids love to say, "attractive."

Think, finally, of Hedda Nussbaum. At times, the debate over how much responsibility she could bear for not pre-

venting the death of six-year-old Lisa Steinberg overshadowed
the fact, which no one outside the courtroom disputed, that
it was Joel Steinberg who caused the child to die. Ms. Nussbaum's warped psyche, her inability to flee a savagely violent
relationship, her inaction the night Lisa lay dying—these are
interesting subjects, endlessly discussed on TV, in the papers,
at the dinner table. But surely they are not *more* interesting
than Steinberg's warped psyche, his descent into brutality and
megalomania. He, too, was a human being with moral choices
to make, a product of the same society that produced Hedda.
But it was she who got the in-depth analysis; what he got was
epithets: "monster," "devil."

We live, I am trying to say, in an epidemic of male violence
against women. But our response to it is almost always to
dismiss the perpetrator with routine expressions of shock and
focus our real attention on the behavior of the victim—usually
to find something wrong with it. We blame Hedda Nussbaum
for not aggressively seeking protection, Lisa Bianco for thinking protection would be effective, Jennifer Levin for thinking
she didn't need any and Karen Straw for protecting herself.
When are we going to apply some of this intense scrutiny to
men?

Consider the latest horror stories served up to us by the
media. The Central Park jogger was chided, at first, for ven-
turing into a deserted area after dark. That aspect of her case,
which would surely have taken center stage had only one
attacker been involved (or had she gone into the park to smoke
a joint, say, or drink some Thunderbird), has been shunted
aside by the sheer gratuitousness of the violence committed,
it seems, by so many kids. And so we talk instead about race,
and class, and television, and adolescence, and the solid, stable
families the kids supposedly come from. We talk about
"wolfpacks" and "wilding." What we don't talk about is the
way this attack upon a woman resembles other, less famous

ones: fraternity gang-rapes, for example (white wilding?), or the daily assaults upon black and Hispanic women in their own neighborhoods.

And then there is the case of John Mack, recently resigned right-hand man of former Speaker of the House Jim Wright. As a young night manager of a shop, John Mack bludgeoned and slashed a woman customer nearly to death. For a variety of reasons, one of them being that he was Representative Wright's daughter's brother-in-law, John Mack was not categorized as a monster or a devil or a wild animal. To the court, which gave him a relatively light sentence, to Wright, who offered him a job and many promotions, to the mostly male politicians on Capitol Hill who accepted him as a colleague and friend despite knowledge of his crime, John Mack was a good guy who had made a "mistake." Some mistake! What, one wonders, was he *trying* to do?

A good guy who makes a mistake may seem poles apart from a monster, but at bottom both categories have the same effect—they distance violence against women from the fabric of daily experience by making it seem unfathomable, bizarre and rare when really it is none of those things. Detach the act from the man by labeling it an anomaly (or a "tragedy"— remember how often we were told that Jennifer Levin's killing was a tragedy for Robert Chambers, too?). When that's impossible, because the act is too gory, or has been repeated too often, detach the man from the male half of humanity by labeling him inhuman.

This kind of thinking gets us worse than nowhere. What we should be asking is not how the most sensational crimes against women are different from run-of-the-mill threats, rapes, bashings and murders but how they are the same. We need to stop thinking of male violence as some kind of freak of nature, like a tornado. Because the thing about tornadoes is, you can't do anything about them. The onus is all on potential victims to accommodate themselves or stay out of the way (What was she wearing? Why was she out so late? Why didn't she flee/scream/fight back/stay calm?).

Could it be, for example, that defining a Joel Steinberg as a monster is mostly a way of not having to think about how he resembles the millions of men who hit but don't kill? That those good guys who astonish everyone when they make a "mistake" only passed for good because we don't take seriously the casual hostility to women such men usually display long before they rape or kill?

Perhaps we are too quick to assume that men who mutter obscenities on the street, or run female joggers off the road with their cars, or cheer the rape scenes in movies, let it stop there. Some of them may be testing the waters, and getting the message that it's clear sailing ahead.

1989

Why I Hate "Family Values"

Unlike many of the commentators who have made Murphy Brown the most famous unmarried mother since Ingrid Bergman ran off with Roberto Rossellini, I actually watched the notorious childbirth episode. After reading my sleep-resistant four-year-old her entire collection of Berenstain Bears books, television was all I was fit for. And that is how I know that I belong to the cultural elite: Not only can I spell "potato" correctly, and the names of many other vegetables as well, I thought the show was a veritable riot of family values. First of all, Murph is smart, warm, playful, decent and rich: She'll be a great mom. Second, the dad is her ex-husband: The baby is as close to legitimate as the scriptwriters could manage, given that Murph is divorced. Third, her ex spurned *her*, not, as Dan Quayle implied, the other way around. Fourth, she rejected abortion. On TV, women have abortions only in docudramas, usually after being raped, drugged with birth-defect-inducing chemicals or put into a coma. Finally, what does Murph sing to the newborn? "You make me feel like a natural woman"! Even on the most feminist sitcom in TV history (if you take points off "Kate and Allie" for never so much as mentioning the word "gay"), anatomy is destiny.

That a show as fluffy and genial as "Murphy Brown" has touched off a national debate about "family values" speaks volumes—and not just about the apparent inability of Dan Quayle to distinguish real life from a TV show. (And since when are sitcom writers part of the cultural elite, anyway? I thought they were the crowd-pleasing lowbrows, and *intellectuals* were the cultural elite.) The "Murphy Brown" debate, it turns out, isn't really about Murphy Brown; it's about inner-city women, who will be encouraged to produce out-of-wedlock babies by Murph's example—the trickle-down theory of values. (Do welfare moms watch "Murphy Brown"? I thought it was supposed to be soap operas, as in "they just sit around all day watching the soaps." Marriage is a major obsession on the soaps—but never mind.) Everybody, it seems, understood this substitution immediately. After all, why get upset about Baby Boy Brown? Is there any doubt that he will be safe, loved, well schooled, taken for checkups, taught to respect the rights and feelings of others and treated to *The Berenstain Bears Visit the Dentist* as often as his little heart desires? Unlike millions of kids who live with both parents, he will never be physically or sexually abused, watch his father beat his mother (domestic assault is the leading cause of injury to women) or cower beneath the blankets while his parents scream at each other. And chances are excellent that he won't sexually assault a retarded girl with a miniature baseball bat, like those high school athletes in posh Glen Ridge, New Jersey; or shoot his lover's spouse, like Amy Fisher; or find himself on trial for rape, like William Kennedy Smith—children of intact and prosperous families every one of them. He'll probably go to Harvard and major in semiotics. Maybe that's the problem. Just think, if Murph were married, like Dan Quayle's mom, he could go to DePauw University and major in golf.

That there is something called "the family"—Papa Bear, Mama Bear, Brother Bear and Sister Bear—that is the best setting for raising children, and that it is in trouble because of a decline in "values," are bromides accepted by commentators of all political stripes. The right blames a left-wing cultural conspiracy: obscene rock lyrics, sex education, abortion, prayerless schools, working mothers, promiscuity, homosexuality, decline of respect for authority and hard work, welfare and, of course, feminism. (On the *Chicago Tribune* Op-Ed page, Allan Carlson, president of the ultraconservative Rockford Institute, found a previously overlooked villain: federal housing subsidies. With all that square footage lying around, singles and unhappy spouses could afford to live on their own.) The left blames the ideology of postindustrial capitalism: consumerism, individualism, selfishness, alienation, lack of social supports for parents and children, atrophied communities, welfare and feminism. The center agonizes over teen sex, welfare moms, crime and divorce, unsure what the causes are beyond some sort of moral failure—probably related to feminism. Interesting how that word keeps coming up.

I used to wonder what family values are. As a matter of fact, I still do. If abortion, according to the right, undermines family values, then single motherhood (as the producers of "Murphy Brown" were quick to point out) must be in accord with them, no? No. Over on the left, if gender equality, love and sexual expressivity are desirable features of contemporary marriage, then isn't marriage bound to be unstable, given how hard those things are to achieve and maintain? Not really.

Just say no, says the right. Try counseling, says the left. Don't be so lazy, says the middle. Indeed, in its guilt-mongering cover story "Legacy of Divorce: How the Fear of Failure Haunts the Children of Broken Marriages," *Newsweek* was unable to come up with any explanation for the high American divorce rate except that people just didn't try hard enough to stay married.

When left, right and center agree, watch out. They probably don't know what they're talking about. And so it is with "the family" and "family values." In the first place, these terms lump together distinct social phenomena that in reality have not very much to do with one another. The handful of forty-something professionals like Murphy Brown who elect to have a child without a male partner have little in common with the millions of middle- and working-class divorced mothers who find themselves in desperate financial straits because their husbands fail to pay court-awarded child support. And neither category has much in common with inner-city girls like those a teacher friend of mine told me about the other day: a thirteen-year-old and a twelve-year-old, impregnated by boyfriends twice their age and determined to bear and keep the babies—to spite abusive parents, to confirm their parents' low opinion of them, to have someone to love who loves them in return.

Beyond that, appeals to "the family" and its "values" frame the discussion as one about morals instead of consequences. In real life, for example, teen sex—the subject of endless sermons—has little relation with teen childbearing. That sounds counterfactual, but it's true. Western European teens have sex about as early and as often as American ones, but are much less likely to have babies. Partly it's because there are far fewer European girls whose lives are as marked by hopelessness and brutality as those of my friend's students. And partly it's because European youth have much better access to sexual information, birth control and abortion. Or consider divorce. In real life, parents divorce for all kinds of reasons, not because they lack moral fiber and are heedless of their children's needs. Indeed, many divorce because they *do* consider their kids, and want to protect them from the poisonous effects of growing up in a household marked by violence, craziness, open verbal warfare or simple lovelessness.

Perhaps this is the place to say that I come to the family-values debate with a personal bias. I am recently separated myself. I think my husband and I would fall under *Newsweek*'s "didn't try harder" rubric, although we thought about splitting up for years, discussed it for almost a whole additional year and consulted no fewer than four therapists, including a marital counselor who advised us that marriage was one of modern humanity's only means of self-transcendence (religion and psychoanalysis were the others, which should have warned me) and admonished us that we risked a future of shallow relationships if we shirked our spiritual mission, not to mention the damage we would "certainly" inflict on our daughter. I thought he was a jackass—shallow relationships? *moi?* But he got to me. Because our marriage wasn't some flaming disaster—with broken dishes and hitting and strange hotel charges showing up on the MasterCard bill. It was just unhappy, in ways that weren't going to change. Still, I think both of us would have been willing to trudge on to spare our child suffering. That's what couples do in women's magazines; that's what the Clintons say they did. But we realized it wouldn't work: As our daughter got older, she would see right through us, the way kids do. And, worse, no matter how hard I tried to put on a happy face, I would wordlessly communicate to her—whose favorite fairy tale is "Cinderella," and whose favorite game is Wedding, complete with bath-towel bridal veil—my resentment and depression and cynicism about relations between the sexes.

The family-values advocates would doubtless say that my husband and I made a selfish choice, which society should have impeded or even prevented. There's a growing sentiment in policy land to make divorce more difficult. In *When the Bough Breaks*, Sylvia Ann Hewlett argues that couples should be forced into therapy (funny how ready people are to believe that counseling, which even when voluntary takes years to modify garden-variety neuroses, can work wonders in months with resistant patients who hate each other). Christopher Lasch briefly supported a constitutional amendment forbidding divorce to couples with minor children, as if lack of a separation agreement would keep people living together (he's backed off that position, he told me recently). The Communitarians, who flood my mailbox with self-promoting worry-fests, furrow their brows wondering "How can the family be saved without forcing women to stay at home or otherwise violating their rights?" (Good luck.) But I am still waiting for someone to explain why it would be better for my daughter to grow up in a joyless household than to live as she does now, with two reasonably cheerful parents living around the corner from each other, both committed to her support and cooperating, as they say on "Sesame Street," in her care. We may not love each other, but we both love her. Maybe that's as much as parents can do for their children, and all that should be asked of them.

But, of course, civilized cooperation is exactly what many divorced parents find they cannot manage. The statistics on deadbeat and vanishing dads are shocking—less than half pay child support promptly and in full, and around half seldom or never see their kids within a few years of marital breakup. Surely, some of this male abdication can be explained by the very thinness of the traditional paternal role worshiped by the preachers of "values"; it's little more than breadwinning, discipline and fishing trips. How many diapers, after all, has Dan Quayle changed? A large percentage of American fathers have never changed a single one. Maybe the reason so many fathers fade away after divorce is that they were never really there to begin with.

It is true that people's ideas about marriage are not what they were in the 1950s—although those who look back at the fifties nostalgically forget both that many of those marriages were miserable and that the fifties were an atypical decade in more than a century of social change. Married women have been moving steadily into the workforce since 1890; beginning even earlier, families have been getting smaller; divorce has been rising; sexual activity has been initiated ever earlier and marriage delayed; companionate marriage has been increasingly accepted as desirable by all social classes and both sexes. It may be that these trends have reached a tipping point, at which they come to define a new norm. Few men expect to marry virgins, and children are hardly "stigmatized" by divorce, as they might have been a mere fifteen or twenty years ago. But if people want different things from family life—if women, as Arlie Hochschild pointed out in *The Second Shift*, cite as a major reason for separation the failure of their husbands to share domestic labor; if both sexes are less willing to resign themselves to a marriage devoid of sexual pleasure, intimacy or shared goals; if single women decide they want to be mothers; if teenagers want to sleep together—why shouldn't society adapt? Society is, after all, just us. Nor are these developments unique to the United States. All over the industrialized world, divorce rates are high, single women are having babies by choice, homosexuals are coming out of the closet and infidelity, always much more common than anyone wanted to recognize, is on the rise. Indeed, in some ways America is behind the rest of the West: We still go to church, unlike the British, the French and, now that Franco is out of the way, the Spanish. More religious than Spain! Imagine.

I'm not saying that these changes are without cost—in poverty, loneliness, insecurity and stress. The reasons for this suffering, however, lie not in moral collapse but in our failure to acknowledge and adjust to changing social relations. We still act as if mothers stayed home with children, wives didn't need to work and men earned a "family wage." We'd rather preach about teenage "promiscuity" than teach young people—especially young women—how to negotiate sexual issues responsibly. If my friend's students had been prepared for puberty by schools and discussion groups and health centers, the way Dutch young people are, they might not have ended up pregnant, victims of what is, after all, statutory rape. And if women earned a dollar for every dollar earned by men, divorce and single parenthood would not mean poverty. Nobody worries about single fathers raising children, after all; indeed, paternal custody is the latest legal fad.

What is the point of trying to put the new wine of modern personal relations in the old bottles of the sexual double standard and lifelong miserable marriage? For that is what most of the current discourse on "family issues" amounts to. No matter how fallacious, the culture greets moralistic approaches to these subjects with instant agreement. Judith Wallerstein's travesty of social science, *Second Chances*, asserts that children are emotionally traumatized by divorce, and the fact that she had no control group is simply ignored by an ecstatic press. As it happens, a 1991 study in *Science* did use a control group. By following 17,000 children for four years, and comparing those whose parents split with those whose parents stayed in troubled marriages, the researchers found that the "divorce effect" disappeared entirely for boys and was very small for girls. Not surprisingly, this study attracted absolutely no attention.

Similarly, we are quick to blame poor unmarried mothers for all manner of social problems—crime, unemployment, drops in reading scores, teen suicide. The solution? Cut off all welfare for additional children. Force teen mothers to live with their parents. Push the women to marry in order to attach them to a male income. (So much for love—talk about marriage as legalized prostitution!)

New Jersey's new welfare reform law gives economic coercion a particularly bizarre twist. Welfare moms who marry can keep part of their dole, but only if the man is *not* the father of their children. The logic is that, married or not, Dad has a financial obligation to his kids, but Mr. Just Got Into Town does not. If the law's inventors are right that welfare policy can micromanage marital and reproductive choice, they have just guaranteed that no woman on the dole will marry her children's father. This is strengthening the family?

Charles Murray, of the American Enterprise Institute, thinks New Jersey does not go far enough. Get rid of welfare entirely, he argued in *The New York Times*: Mothers should marry or starve, and if they are foolish enough to prefer the latter, their kids should be put up for adoption or into orphanages. Mickey Kaus, who favors compulsory low-wage employment for the poor, likes orphanages, too.

None of those punitive approaches will work. There is no evidence that increased poverty decreases family size, and welfare moms aren't likely to meet many men with family-size incomes, or they'd probably be married already, though maybe not for long. The men who impregnated those seventh graders, for example, are much more likely to turn them out as prostitutes than to lead them to the altar. For one thing, those men may well be married already.

The fact is, the harm connected with the dissolution of "the family" is not a problem of values—at least not individual values—it's a problem of money. When there are no jobs and the poor are abandoned to their fates, people don't get to display "work ethic," don't feel good about themselves and don't marry or stay married. The girls don't have anything to postpone motherhood for; the boys have no economic prospects that would make them reasonable marriage partners. This was true in the slums of eighteenth-century London, and it is true today in the urban slums of Latin America and Africa, as well as in those of the United States. Or take divorce. Of course divorce can be psychologically hard on children, and on their parents, too. But social policy can't do very much about that, any more than it can make a bad marriage a good one. What government can do something about is the economic consequences of divorce: It makes lots of women, and their children, poor. One reason, which has got a fair amount of attention recently, is the scandalously low level of child support, plus the tendency of courts to award a disproportionate share of the marital assets to the man. The other reason is that women earn much less than men, thanks to gender discrimination and the failure of the workplace to adapt to the needs of working mothers. Instead of moaning about "family values" we should be thinking about how to provide the poor with decent jobs and social services, and about how to insure economic justice for working women. And let marriage take care of itself.

Family values and the cult of the nuclear family is, at bottom, just another way to bash women, especially poor women. If only they would get married and stay married, society's ills would vanish. Inner-city crime would disappear because fathers would communicate manly values to their sons, which would cause jobs to spring up like mushrooms after rain. Welfare would fade away. Children would do well in school. (Irene Impellizeri, anticondom vice president of the New York City Board of Education, recently gave a speech attributing inner-city children's poor grades and high dropout rates to the failure of their families to provide "moral models," the way immigrant parents did in the good old days—a dangerous argument for her, in particular, to make; doesn't she know that Italian-American kids have dropout and failure rates only slightly lower than black and Latino teens?)

When pundits preach morality, I often find myself thinking of Samuel Johnson, literature's greatest enemy of cant and fatuity. What would the eighteenth-century moralist make of our current obsession with marriage? "Sir," he replied to Boswell, who held that marriage was a natural state, "it is so far from being natural for a man and woman to live in the state of marriage that we find all the motives which they have for remaining in that connection, and the restraints which civilized society imposes to prevent separation, are hardly sufficient to keep them together." Dr. Johnson knew what he was talking about: He and his wife lived apart. And what would he think of our confusion of moral preachments with practical solutions to social problems? Remember his response to Mrs. Thrale's long and flowery speech on the cost of children's clothes. "Nay, madam," he said, "when you are declaiming, declaim; and when you are calculating, calculate."

Which is it going to be? Declamation, which feeds no children, employs no jobless and reduces gender relations to an economic bargain? Or calculation, which accepts the fact that the Berenstain Bears, like Murphy Brown, are fiction? The people seem to be voting with their feet on "the family." It's time for our "values" to catch up.

1992

Marooned on Gilligan's Island: Are Women Morally Superior to Men?

S ome years ago, I was invited by the wife of a well-known writer to sign a women's peace petition. It made the points such documents usually make: that women, as mothers, caregivers and nurturers, have a special awareness of the precariousness of human life, see through jingoism and Cold War rhetoric and would prefer nations to work out their difficulties peacefully so that the military budget could be diverted to schools and hospitals and housing. It had the literary tone such documents usually have, as well—at once superior and plaintive, as if the authors didn't know whether they were bragging or begging. We are wiser than you poor deluded menfolk, was the subtext, so will you please-please-please listen to your moms?

To sign or not to sign? Of course, I was all for peace. But was I for peace *as a woman*? I wasn't a mother then—I wasn't even an aunt. Did my lack of nurturing credentials make my grasp of the horrors of war and the folly of the arms race only theoretical, like a white person's understanding of racism? Were mothers the natural leaders of the peace movement, to whose judgment nonmothers, male and female, must defer, because after all we couldn't *know*, couldn't *feel* that tenderness toward fragile human life that a woman who had borne and raised children had experienced? On the other hand, I was indeed a woman. Was motherhood with its special wisdom somehow deep inside me, to be called upon when needed, like my uterus?

Complicating matters in a way relevant to this essay was my response to the famous writer's wife herself. Here was a woman in her fifties, her child-raising long behind her. Was motherhood the only banner under which she could gain a foothold on civic life? Perhaps so. Her only other public identity was that of a wife, and wifehood, even to a famous man, isn't much to claim credit for these days. ("To think I spent all those years ironing his underpants!" she once burst out to a mutual friend.) Motherhood was what she had in the work-and-accomplishment department, so it was understandable that she try to maximize its moral status. But I was not in her situation: I was a writer, a single woman. By sending me a petition from which I was excluded even as I was invited to add my name, perhaps she was telling me that by leading a nondomestic life I had abandoned the moral high ground, was "acting like a man," but could redeem myself by acknowledging the moral preeminence of the class of women I refused to join.

The ascription of particular virtues—compassion, patience, common sense, nonviolence—to mothers, and the tendency to conflate "mothers" with "women," has a long history in the peace movement, but it goes way beyond issues of war and peace. At present it permeates discussions of just about every field, from management training to theology. Indeed, although the media like to caricature feminism as denying the existence of sexual differences, for the women's movement and its opponents alike "difference" is where the action is. Thus, business writers wonder if women's nurturing, intuitive qualities will make them better executives. Educators suggest that female students suffer in classrooms that emphasize competition over cooperation. Women politicians tout their playground-honed negotiating skills, their egoless devotion to public service, their gender-based commitment to fairness and caring. A variety of political causes—environmentalism, animal rights, even vegetarianism—are promoted as logical extensions of women's putative peacefulness, closeness to nature, horror of aggression and concern for others' health. (Indeed, to some extent these causes are arenas in which women fight one another over definitions of femininity, which is why debates over disposable diapers and over the wearing of fur— both rather minor sources of harm, even if their opponents are right—loom so large and are so acrimonious.) In the arts, we hear a lot about what women's "real" subjects, methods and materials ought to be. Painting is male. Rhyme is male. Plot is male. Perhaps, say the Lacanian feminists, even logic and language are male. What is female? Nature. Blood. Milk. Communal gatherings. The moon. Quilts.

Haven't we been here before? Indeed we have. Woman as sharer and carer, woman as earth mother, woman as guardian of all the small rituals that knit together a family and a community, woman as beneath, above or beyond such manly concerns as law, reason, abstract ideas—these images are as old as time. Open defenders of male supremacy have always used them to declare women flatly inferior to men; covert ones use them to place women on a pedestal as too good for this naughty world. Thus, in the *Eumenides*, Aeschylus celebrated law as the defeat by males of primitive female principles of bloodguilt and vengeance, while the Ayatollah Khomeini thought women should be barred from judgeships because they were too tenderhearted. Different rationale, same outcome: Women, because of their indifference to an impersonal moral order, cannot be full participants in civic life.

There exists an equally ancient line of thought, however, that uses femininity to posit a subversive challenge to the social order: Think of Sophocles' Antigone, who resists tyranny out of love and piety, or Aristophanes' Lysistrata, the original women's-strike-for-peace-nik, or Shakespeare's unworldly, loving innocents: Desdemona, Cordelia. For reasons of power, money and persistent social structures, the vision of the morally superior woman can never overcome the dominant ethos in reality but exists alongside it as a kind of permanent wish or hope: If only powerful and powerless could change places, and the meek inherit the earth! Thus, it is perpetually being rediscovered, dressed in fashionable clothes and presented, despite its antiquity, as a radical new idea.

In the 1950s, which we think of as the glory days of traditional sex roles, the anthropologist Ashley Montagu argued in "The Natural Superiority of Women" that females had it all over males in every way that counted, including the possession of two X chromosomes that made them stabler, saner and healthier than men, with their X and Y. Montagu's essay, originally published in *The Saturday Review* and later expanded into a book, is witty and high-spirited and, interestingly, anticipates the current feminist challenge to male-defined categories. (He notes, for example, that while men are stronger than women in the furniture-moving sense, women are stronger than men when faced with extreme physical hardship and tests of endurance; so when we say that men are stronger than women, we are equating strength with what men have.) But the fundamental thrust of Montagu's essay was to confirm traditional gender roles while revising the way we value them. Having proved to his own satisfaction that women could scale the artistic and intellectual heights, he argued that most would (that is, should) refrain, because women's true genius was "humanness," and their real mission was to "humanize" men before men blew up the world. And that, he left no doubt, was a full-time job.

Contemporary proponents of "difference feminism" advance a variation on the same argument, without Montagu's puckish humor. Instead of his whimsical chromosomal explanation, we get, for example, the psychoanalytic one proposed by Nancy Chodorow in *The Reproduction of Mothering*: Daughters define themselves by relating to their mothers, the primary love object of all children, and are therefore empathic, relationship-oriented, nonhierarchical and interested in forging consensus; sons must separate from their mothers, and are therefore individualistic, competitive, resistant to connection with others and focused on abstract rules and rights. Chodorow's theory has become a kind of mantra of difference feminism, endlessly cited as if it explained phenomena we all agree are universal, though this is far from the case. The central question Chodorow poses—Why are women the primary caregivers of children?—could not even be asked before the advent of modern birth control, and can be answered without resorting to psychology. Historically, women have taken care of children because high fertility and lack of other options left most of them no choice. Those rich enough to avoid personally raising their children often did, as Rousseau observed to his horror.

Popularizers of Chodorow water down and sentimentalize her thesis. They embrace her proposition that traditional mothering produces "relational" women and "autonomous" men but forget her less congenial argument that it also results in sexual inequality, misogyny and hostility between mothers and daughters, who, like sons, desire independence but have a much harder time achieving it. Unlike her followers, Chodorow does not romanticize mothering: "Exclusive single parenting is bad for mother and child alike," she concludes; in a tragic paradox, female "caring," "intimacy" and "nurturance" do not soften but *produce* aggressive, competitive, hypermasculine men.

The relational woman and autonomous man described in psychoanalytic terms by Chodorow have become stock figures in other areas of social science as well. Thus, in her immensely influential book, *In a Different Voice*, the educational psychologist Carol Gilligan argues that the sexes make moral decisions according to separate criteria: Women employ an "ethic of care," men an "ethic of rights." The sociolinguist Deborah Tannen, in the best-selling *You Just Don't Understand*, analyzes male-female conversation as "cross-cultural communication" by people from different backgrounds: the single-sex world of children's play in which girls cooperate and boys compete. While these two writers differ in important ways—Tannen, writing at a more popular level, is by far the clearer thinker and the one more interested in analyzing actual human interactions in daily life, about which she is often quite shrewd— they share important liabilities, too. Both largely confine their observations to the white middle class—especially Gilligan, much of whose elaborate theory of gendered ethics rests on interviews with a handful of Harvard-Radcliffe undergraduates—and seem unaware that this limits the applicability of their data. (In their 1992 book, *Meeting at the Crossroads*, Gilligan and her co-author, Lyn Mikel Brown, make a similar mistake. Their whole theory of "loss of relationship" as the central trauma of female adolescence rests on interviews with students at one posh single-sex private school.) Both massage their findings to fit their theories: Gilligan's male and female responses are actually quite similar to each other, as experimenters have subsequently shown by removing the names and asking subjects to try to sort the answers by gender; Tannen is quick to attribute blatant rudeness or sexism in male speech to anxiety, helplessness, fear of loss of face—to anything, indeed, but rudeness and sexism. Both look only at what people say, not what they do. For Tannen this isn't a decisive objection because speech is her subject, although it limits the extent to which her findings can be applied to other areas of behavior; for Gilligan, it is a major obstacle, unless you believe, as she apparently does, that the way people say they would resolve farfetched hypothetical dilemmas—Should a poor man steal drugs to save his dying wife?—tells us how they reason in real-life situations or, more important, how they act.

But the biggest problem with all these accounts of gender difference is that they credit the differences they find to universal features of male and female development rather than to the economic and social positions men and women hold, or to the actual power differences between individual men and women. In *The Mismeasure of Woman*, her trenchant and witty attack on contemporary theories of gender difference, Carol Tavris points out that much of what can be said about women applies as well to poor people, who also tend to focus more on family and relationships and less on work and self-advancement; to behave deferentially with those more socially powerful; and to appear to others more emotional and "intuitive" than rational and logical in their thinking. Then, too, there is the question of whether the difference theorists are measuring anything beyond their own willingness to think in stereotypes. If Chodorow is right, relational women and autonomous men should be the norm, but are they? Or is it just that women and men use different language, have different social styles, offer different explanations for similar behavior? Certainly, it is easy to find in one's own acquaintance, as well as in the world at large, men and women who don't fit the models. Difference feminists like to attribute ruthlessness, coldness and hyperrationality in successful women—Margaret Thatcher is the standard example—to the fact that men control the networks of power and permit only women like themselves to rise. But I've met plenty of rigid, insensitive, aggressive women who are stay-at-home mothers and secretaries and nurses. And I know plenty of sweet, unambitious men whose main satisfactions lie in their social, domestic and romantic lives, although not all of them would admit this to an inquiring social scientist. We tend to tell strangers what we think will make us sound good. I myself, to my utter amazement, informed a telephone pollster that I exercised regularly, a bare-faced lie. How much more difficult to describe truthfully one's moral and ethical values—even if one knew what they were, which, as Socrates demonstrated at length, almost no one does.

So why are Gilligan and Tannen the toasts of feminist social science, endlessly cited and discussed in academia, and out of it too, in gender-sensitivity sessions in the business world and even, following the Anita Hill–Clarence Thomas hearings, in Congress? The success of the difference theorists proves yet again that social science is one part science and nine parts social. They say what people want to hear: Women really are different, in just the ways we always thought. Women embrace Gilligan and Tannen because they offer flattering accounts of traits for which they have historically been castigated. Men like them because, while they urge understanding and respect for "female" values and behaviors, they also let men off the hook: Men have power, wealth and control of social resources because women don't really want them. The pernicious tendencies of difference feminism are perfectly illustrated by the Sears sex discrimination case, in which Rosalind Rosenberg, a professor of women's history at Barnard College, testified for Sears that female employees held lower-paying salaried jobs while men worked selling big-ticket items on commission because women preferred low-risk, noncompetitive positions that did not interfere with family responsibilities. Sears won its case.

While early-childhood development is the point of departure for most of the difference feminists, it is possible to construct a theory of gendered ethics on other grounds. The most interesting attempt I've seen is by the pacifist philosopher Sara Ruddick. Although not widely known outside academic circles, her *Maternal Thinking* makes an argument that can be found in such mainstream sources as the columns of Anna Quindlen in *The New York Times*. For Ruddick it is not psychosexual development that produces the Gilliganian virtues but intimate involvement in child-raising, the hands-on work of mothering. Men too can be mothers if they do the work that women do. (And women can be Fathers—a word Ruddick uses, complete with arrogant capital letter, for distant, uninvolved authority-figure parents.) Mothers are patient, peace-loving, attentive to emotional context and so on, because those are the qualities you need to get the job done, the way accountants are precise, lawyers argumentative, writers self-centered. Thus mothers constitute a logical constituency for pacifist and antiwar politics, and, by extension, a "caring" domestic agenda.

But what is the job of mothering? Ruddick defines "maternal practice" as meeting three demands: preservation, growth and social acceptability. She acknowledges the enormously varying manifestations of these demands, but she doesn't incorporate into her theory the qualifications, limits and contradictions she notes—perhaps because to do so would reveal these demands as so flexible as to be practically empty terms.

Almost anything mothers do can be explained under one of these rubrics, however cruel, dangerous, unfair or authoritarian—the genital mutilation of African and Arab girls, the foot-binding of prerevolutionary Chinese ones, the sacrifice of some children to increase the resources available for others, as in the killing or malnourishing of female infants in India and China today. In this country, many mothers who commit what is legally child abuse *think* they are merely disciplining their kids in the good old-fashioned way. As long as the practices are culturally acceptable (and sometimes even when they're not), the mothers who perform them think of themselves as good parents. But if all these behaviors count as mothering, how can mothering have a necessary connection with any single belief about anything, let alone how to stop war, or any single set of personality traits, let alone nonviolent ones?

We should not be surprised that motherhood does not produce uniform beliefs and behaviors: It is, after all, not a job; it has no standard of admission, and almost nobody gets fired. Motherhood is open to any woman who can have a baby or adopt one. *Not* to be a mother is a decision; becoming one requires merely that a woman accede, perhaps only for as long as it takes to get pregnant, to thousands of years of cumulative social pressure. After that, she's on her own; she can soothe her child's nightmares or let him cry in the dark. Nothing intrinsic to child-raising will tell her what is the better choice for her child (each has been the favored practice at different times). Although Ruddick starts off by looking closely at maternal practice, when that practice contradicts her own ideas about good mothering it is filed away as an exception, a distortion imposed by Fathers or poverty or some other outside force. But if you add up all the exceptions, you are left with a rather small group of people—women like Ruddick herself, enlightened, up-to-date, educated, upper-middle-class liberals.

And not even all of them. Consider the issue of physical punishment. Ruddick argues that experience teaches mothers that violence is useless; it only creates anger, deception and more violence. Negotiation is the mother's way of resolving disputes and encouraging good behavior. As Ann Crittenden put it in *The Nation* during the Gulf War: "One learns, in theory and in practice, to try to resolve conflict in ways that do not involve the sheer imposition of will or brute force. One learns that violence just doesn't work." Crittenden would have a hard time explaining all those moms in uniform who participated in Operation Desert Storm—but then she'd have a hard time explaining all those mothers screaming at their kids in the supermarket, too.

As it happens, I agree that violence is a bad way to teach, and I made a decision never, no matter what, to spank my daughter. But mothers who do not hit their children, or permit their husbands to do so, are as rare as conscientious objectors in wartime. According to one survey, 78 percent approve of an occasional "good, hard spanking"—because they think violence *is* an effective way of teaching, because they think that hitting children isn't really violence, because they just lose it. Even *Parenting* found that more than a third of its readers hit their kids. And *Parenting*'s audience is not only far more educated, affluent and liberal than the general population, it consists entirely of people who care what experts think about child development—and contemporary experts revile corporal punishment. Interestingly, the moms who hit tended to be the ones who fretted the most about raising their children well. Mothers who think too much?

Like old-style socialists finding "proletarian virtue" in the working class, Ruddick claims to be describing what mothers do, but all too often she is really prescribing what she thinks they ought to do. "When their children flourish, almost all mothers have a sense of well-being." Hasn't she ever heard of postpartum depression? Of mothers who belittle their children's accomplishments and resent their growing independence? "What mother wouldn't want the power to keep her children healthy . . . to create hospitals, schools, jobs, day care, and work schedules that serve her maternal work?" Notice how neatly the modest and commonsensical wish for a healthy child balloons into the hotly contested and by no means universal wish of mothers for day care and flextime. Notice, too, how Ruddick moves from a mother's desire for social institutions that serve *her* children to an assumption that this desire translates into wanting comparable care for *all* children. But mothers feature prominently in local struggles against busing, mergers of rich and poor schools and the opening in their neighborhoods of group homes for foster children, boarder babies and the retarded. Why? The true reasons may be property values and racism, but what these mothers often say is that they are simply protecting their kids. Ruddick seems to think Maternal Thinking leads naturally to Sweden; in the United States it is equally likely to lead to Fortress Suburbia.

As Gilligan does with all women, Ruddick scrutinizes mothers for what she expects to find, and sure enough, there it is. But why look to mothers for her peaceful constituency in the first place? Why not health professionals, who spend their lives saving lives? Or historians, who know how rarely war yields a benefit remotely commensurate with its cost in human misery? Or, I don't know, gardeners, blamelessly tending their innocent flowers? You can read almost any kind of work as affirming life and conferring wisdom. Ruddick chooses mothering because she's already decided that women possess the Gilliganian virtues and she wants a non-essentialist peg to hang them on, so that men can acquire them, too. A disinterested observer scouring the world for labor that encourages humane values would never pick child-raising: It's too quirky, too embedded in repellent cultural norms, too hot.

Despite its intellectual flabbiness, difference feminism is deeply appealing to many women. Why? For one thing, it seems to explain some important phenomena: that women—and this is a cross-cultural truth—commit very little criminal violence compared with men; that women fill the ranks of the so-called caring professions; that women are much less likely than men to abandon their children. Difference feminists want to give women credit for these good behaviors by raising them from the level of instinct or passivity—the Camille Paglia vision of femininity—to the level of moral choice and principled decision. Who can blame women for embracing theories that tell them the sacrifices they make on behalf of domesticity and children are legitimate, moral, even noble? By stressing the mentality of nurturance—the *ethic* of caring, maternal *thinking*—Gilligan and Ruddick challenge the ancient division of humanity into rational males and irrational females. They offer women a way to argue that their views have equal status with those of men and to resist the customary marginalization of their voices in public debate. Doubtless many women have felt emboldened by Gilliganian accounts of moral difference: Speaking in a different voice is, after all, a big step up from silence.

The vision of women as sharers and carers is tempting in another way, too. Despite much media blather about the popularity of the victim position, most people want to believe they act out of free will and choice. The uncomfortable truth that women have all too little of either is a difficult hurdle for feminists. Acknowledging the systematic oppression of women seems to deprive them of existential freedom, to turn them into puppets, slaves and Stepford wives. Deny it, and you can't make change. By arguing that the traditional qualities, tasks and ways of life of women are as important, valuable and serious as those of men (if not more so), Gilligan and others let women feel that nothing needs to change except the social valuation accorded to what they are already doing. It's a rationale for the status quo, which is why men like it, and a burst of grateful applause, which is why women like it. Men keep the power, but since power is bad, so much the worse for them.

Another rather curious appeal of difference feminism is that it offers a way for women to define themselves as independent of men. In a culture that sees women almost entirely in relation to men, this is no small achievement. Sex, for example—the enormous amount of female energy, money and time spent on beauty and fashion and romance, on attracting men and keeping them, on placating male power, strategizing ways around it or making it serve one's own ends—plays a minute role in these theories. You would never guess from Gilligan or Ruddick that men, individually and collectively, are signal beneficiaries of female nurturance, much less that this goes far to explain why society encourages nurturance in women. No, it is always children whom women are described as fostering and sacrificing for, or the community, or even other women—not husbands or lovers. It's as though wives cook dinner only for their kids, leaving the husband to raid the fridge on his own. And no doubt many a woman, quietly smoldering at her mate's refusal to share domestic labor, persuades herself that she is serving only her children, or her own preferences, rather than confront the inequality of her marriage.

The peaceful mother and the relational woman are a kinder, gentler, leftish version of "family values," and both are modern versions of the separate-spheres ideology of the Victorians. In the nineteenth century, too, some women tried to turn the ideology of sexual difference on its head and expand the moral claims of motherhood to include the public realm. Middle-class women became social reformers, abolitionists, temperance advocates, settlement workers and even took paying jobs in the "helping professions"—nursing, social work, teaching—which were perceived as extensions of women's domestic role although practiced mostly by single women. These women did not deny that their sex fitted them for the home, but argued that domesticity did not end at the front door of the house, or confine itself to dusting (or telling the housemaid to dust). Even the vote could be cast as an extension of domesticity: Women, being more moral than men, would purify the government of vice and corruption, end war and make America safe for family life. (The persistence of this metaphor came home to me when I attended a Women's Action Coalition demonstration during the 1992 Democratic National Convention. There—along with WAC's funny and ferocious all-in-black drum corps and contingents of hip downtown artists brandishing Barbara Kruger posters and shouting slogans like "We're Women! We're Angry! We're Not Going Shopping!"—was a trio of street performers with housecoats and kerchiefs over black catsuits and spiky hair, pushing brooms: Women will clean up government!)

The separate-spheres ideology had obvious advantages for middle-class women in an era when they were formally barred from higher education, political power and most jobs that paid a living wage. But its defects are equally obvious. It defined all women by a single standard, and one developed by a sexist society. It offered women no way to enter jobs that could not be defined as extensions of their domestic roles—you could be a math teacher but not a mathematician, a secretary but not a sea captain—and no way to challenge any but the grossest abuses of male privilege. Difference feminists are making a similar bid for power on behalf of women today, and are caught in similar contradictions. Once again, women are defined by their family roles. Child-raising is seen as woman's glory and joy and opportunity for self-transcendence, while Dad naps on the couch. Women who do not fit the stereotype are castigated as unfeminine—nurses nurture, doctors do not—and domestic labor is romanticized and sold to women as a badge of moral worth.

For all the many current explanations of perceived moral difference between the sexes, one hears remarkably little about the material basis of the family. Yet the motherhood and womanhood being valorized cannot be considered apart from questions of power, privilege and money. There is a reason a non-earning woman can proudly call herself a "wife and mother" and a non-earning man is just unemployed: The traditional female role, with its attendant real or imagined traits and values, implies a male income. Middle-class women go to great lengths to separate themselves from this uncomfortable fact. One often hears married mothers defend their decision to stay at home by heaping scorn on paid employment—caricatured as making widgets or pushing papers or dressing for success —and the difference feminists, too, like to distinguish between altruistic, poorly paid female jobs and the nasty, profitable ones performed by men. In *Prisoners of Men's Dreams*, Suzanne Gordon comes close to blaming the modest status of jobs like nursing and flight attending on women's entry into jobs like medicine and piloting, as if before the women's movement those female-dominated occupations were respected and rewarded. (Nurses should be glad the field no longer has a huge captive labor pool of women: The nursing shortage has led to dramatic improvements in pay, benefits and responsibility. Now nurses earn a man-size income, and men are applying to nursing school in record numbers—exactly what Gordon wants.) It's all very well for some women to condemn others for "acting like men"—i.e., being ambitious, assertive, interested in money and position. But if their husbands did not "act like men," where would they be? Jean Bethke Elshtain, who strenuously resists the notion of gendered ethics, nevertheless bemoans the loss to their communities when women leave volunteering and informal mutual support networks for paid employment. But money must come from somewhere; if women leave to men the job of earning the family income (an option fewer and fewer families can afford), they will be economically dependent on their husbands, a situation that, besides carrying obvious risks in an age of frequent divorce, weakens their bargaining position in the family and insures that men will largely control major decisions affecting family life.

Difference theorists would like to separate out the aspects of traditional womanhood that they approve of and speak only of those. But the parts they like (caring, nurturing, intimacy) are inseparable from the parts they don't like (economic dependence and the subordination of women within the family). The difference theorists try to get around this by positing a world that contains two cultures—a female world of love and ritual and a male world of getting and spending and killing—which mysteriously share a single planet. That vision is expressed neatly in a recent pop-psychology title, *Men Are From Mars, Women Are From Venus*. It would be truer to say men are from Illinois and women are from Indiana—different, sure, but not in ways that have much ethical consequence.

The truth is, there is only one culture, and it shapes each sex in distinct but mutually dependent ways in order to reproduce itself. To the extent that the stereotypes are true, women have the "relational" domestic qualities *because* men have the "autonomous" qualities required to survive and prosper in modern capitalism. She needs a wage earner (even if she has a job, thanks to job discrimination), and he needs someone to mind his children, hold his hand and have his

emotions for him. This—not, as Gordon imagines, some trea-
son to her sex—explains why women who move into male
sectors act very much like men: If they didn't, they'd find
themselves back home in a jiffy. The same necessities and
pressures affect them as affect the men who hold those jobs.
Because we are in a transition period, in which many women
were raised with modest expectations and much emphasis on
the need to please others, social scientists who look for it can
find traces of empathy, caring and so on in some women who
have risen in the world of work and power. But when they
tell us that women doctors will transform American medicine,
or women executives will transform the corporate world, they
are looking backward, not forward. If women really do enter
the workforce on equal terms with men—if they become 50
percent of all lawyers, politicians, car dealers and prison
guards—they may be less sexist (although the example of
Soviet doctors, a majority of them female, is not inspiring
to those who know about the brutal gynecological customs
prevailing in the former U.S.S.R.). And they may bring
with them a distinct set of manners, a separate social style.
But they won't be, in some general way, more honest, kind,
egalitarian, empathic or indifferent to profit. To argue otherwise is to believe that the reason factory owners bust unions,
doctors refuse Medicaid patients and New York City school
custodians don't mop the floors is because they are men.

The ultimate paradox of difference feminism is that it has
come to the fore at a moment when the lives of the sexes are
becoming less distinct than they ever have been in the West.
Look at the decline of single-sex education (researchers may
tout the benefits of all-female schools and colleges, but girls
overwhelmingly choose coeducation); the growth of female
athletics; the virtual abolition of virginity as a requirement for
girls; the equalization of college-attendance rates of males and
females; the explosion of employment for married women and

mothers even of small children; the crossing of workplace gender lines by both females and males; the cultural pressure on men to be warm and active fathers, to do at least some housework, to choose mates who are their equals in education and income potential.

It's fashionable these days to talk about the backlash against equality feminism—I talk this way myself when I'm feeling blue—but equality feminism has scored amazing successes. It has transformed women's expectations in every area of their lives. However, it has not yet transformed society to meet those expectations. The workplace still discriminates. On the home front few men practice egalitarianism, although many preach it; single mothers—and given the high divorce rate, every mother is potentially a single mother—lead incredibly difficult lives.

In this social context, difference feminism is essentially a way for women both to take advantage of equality feminism's success and to accommodate themselves to its limits. It appeals to particular kinds of women—those in the "helping professions" or the home, for example, rather than those who want to be bomber pilots or neurosurgeons or electricians. At the popular level, it encourages women who feel disadvantaged or demeaned by equality to direct their anger against women who have benefited from it by thinking of them as gender traitors and of themselves as suffering for their virtue—thus the hostility of some nurses toward female doctors, and of some stay-at-home mothers toward employed mothers.

For its academic proponents, the appeal lies elsewhere: Difference feminism is a way to carve out a safe space in the face of academia's resistance to female advancement. It works much like multiculturalism, making an end run around a static and discriminatory employment structure by creating an intellectual niche that can be filled only by members of the discriminated-against group. And like other forms of multi-culturalism, it looks everywhere for its explanatory force—biology, psychology, sociology, cultural identity—*except* economics. The difference feminists cannot say that the differences between men and women are the result of their relative economic positions, because to say that would be to move the whole discussion out of the realm of psychology and feel-good cultural pride and into the realm of a tough political struggle over the distribution of resources and justice and money.

Although it is couched in the language of praise, difference feminism is demeaning to women. It asks that women be admitted into public life and public discourse not because they have a right to be there but because they will improve them. Even if this were true, and not the wishful thinking I believe it to be, why should the task of moral and social transformation be laid on women's doorstep and not on everyone's—or, for that matter, on men's, by the you-broke-it-you-fix-it principle? Peace, the environment, a more humane workplace, economic justice, social support for children—these are issues that affect us all and are everyone's responsibility. By promising to assume that responsibility, difference feminists lay the ground-work for excluding women again, as soon as it becomes clear that the promise cannot be kept.

No one asks that other oppressed groups win their freedom by claiming to be extra-good. And no other oppressed group thinks it must make such a claim in order to be accommodated fully and across the board by society. For blacks and other racial minorities, it is enough to want to earn a living, exercise one's talents, get a fair hearing in the public forum. Only for women is simple justice an insufficient argument. It is as though women don't really believe they are entitled to full citizenship unless they can make a special claim to virtue. Why isn't being human enough?

In the end, I didn't sign that peace petition, although I was sorry to disappoint a woman I liked, and although I am very much for peace. I decided to wait for a petition that welcomed my signature as a person, an American, a citizen implicated, against my will, in war and the war economy. I still think I did the right thing.

1992

Contracts and Apple Pie:
The Strange Case of Baby M

I think I understand Judge Harvey Sorkow's ruling in the Baby M case. It seems that a woman can rent her womb in the state of New Jersey, although not her vagina, and get a check upon turning over the product to its father. This transaction is not baby selling (a crime), because a man has a "drive to procreate" that deserves the utmost respect and, in any case, the child is genetically half his. The woman he pays for help in fulfilling that drive, however, is only "performing a service" and thus has no comparable right to a child genetically half hers. Therefore, despite the law's requirements in what the layperson might think are similar cases (women who change their minds about giving up a child for adoption, for example), a judge may terminate a repentant mother-for-money's parental rights forever without finding that she abused or neglected her child—especially if he finds her "manipulative, exploitive or deceitful." In other words, so-called surrogacy agreements are so unprecedented that the resulting human arrangements cannot be likened to adoption, illegitimacy, custody after divorce or any other relationship involving parents and children, yet, at the same time, bear an uncanny resemblance to the all-sales-final style of a used-car lot.

The State Supreme Court will hear Mary Beth White-head's appeal in September and has meanwhile granted her two hours of visiting time a week—a small sign, perhaps, that in jettisoning the entire corpus of family law, Judge Sorkow may have gone a bit too far. (*The New York Times* had trouble finding a single legal scholar who supported the judge's reasoning in full.) Maybe not, though. Despite the qualms of pundits, the outrage of many feminists and the condemnation of many religious leaders, every poll to date has shown overwhelming approval of Judge Sorkow's ruling. Twenty-seven states are considering bills that would legalize and regulate bucks-for-baby deals. What on earth is going on here?

Some of this support surely comes from the bad impression Mrs. Whitehead made every time she opened her mouth—most damningly, in her tape-recorded threat to kill Baby M and herself. And some comes from the inexpertness of her lawyer. (Where was the National Organization for Women? Where was the American Civil Liberties Union?) The Sterns said they would drag the Whiteheads through the mud, and they did. We learned as much about the Whiteheads' marital troubles, financial woes and quarrelsome relatives as if they were characters on "All My Children." Distinguished experts testified that Mrs. Whitehead, who has raised two healthy, normal kids, is a bad mother and emotionally unbalanced: She was "overenmeshed" with her kids, disputed the judgment of school officials, gave Baby M teddy bears to play with instead of pots and pans (*pots and pans?*) and said "hooray" instead of "patty-cake" when the tot clapped her hands. I know that, along with two-thirds of the adult female population of the

United States, I will never feel quite the same about dyeing my hair now that Dr. Marshall Schecter, professor of child psychiatry at the University of Pennsylvania, has cited this little beauty secret as proof of Mrs. Whitehead's "narcissism" and "mixed personality disorder." Will I find myself in custody court someday, faced with the damning evidence of Exhibit A: a half-empty bottle of Clairol's Nice 'n Easy?

Inexplicably, Mrs. Whitehead's lawyer never challenged the Sterns' self-representation as a stable, sane, loving pair, united in their devotion to Baby M. And neither did the media. Thus, we never found out why Dr. Elizabeth Stern claimed to be infertile on her application to the Infertility Center of New York when, in fact, she had diagnosed herself as having multiple sclerosis, which she feared pregnancy would aggravate; or why she didn't confirm that diagnosis until shortly before the case went to trial, much less consult a specialist in the management of M.S. pregnancies. Could it be that Elizabeth Stern did not share her husband's zeal for procreation? We'll never know, any more than we'll know why a disease serious enough to bar pregnancy was not also serious enough to consider as a possible bar to active mothering a few years down the road. If the Sterns' superior income could count as a factor in determining "the best interests of the child," why couldn't Mary Beth Whitehead's superior health?

The trial was so riddled with psychobabble, class prejudice and sheer callousness that one would have expected public opinion to rally round Mrs. Whitehead. Imagine openly arguing that a child should go to the richer parent! (Mrs. Whitehead is a homemaker and her husband drives a garbage truck; Dr. Stern is a professor of pediatrics, and Mr. Stern is a biochemist.) And castigating a mother faced with the loss of her baby as hyperemotional because she wept! But Mrs. Whitehead (who, it must be said, did not help her case by perjuring herself repeatedly) made a fatal mistake: She fell afoul of the double standard of sexual morality. Thus, in the popular mind, Mrs. Whitehead was "an adult" who "knew what she was doing," while Mr. Stern, presumably, was not an adult and did not know what he was doing. Mrs. Whitehead was mercenary for agreeing to sell, but not Mr. Stern for proposing to buy.

The personalities of the Whiteheads and the Sterns, so crucial during the custody phase of the trial, will soon fade from public memory. The extraordinary welter of half-truths, bad analogies, logical muddles and glib catch phrases that have been mustered in defense of their bargain are apparently here to stay. If we really are about to embark on an era of reproductive Reaganomics—and most Americans seem to be saying, Why not?—we at least ought to clear away some of the more blatantly foolish things being said in support of it. For example:

Mary Beth Whitehead is a surrogate mother. "Mother" describes the relationship of a woman to a child, not to the father of that child and his wife. Everything a woman does to produce her own child Mary Beth Whitehead did, including giving it half the genetic inheritance regarded by the judge as so decisive an argument on behalf of William Stern. If anyone was a surrogate mother, it was Elizabeth Stern, for she was the one who substituted, or wished to substitute, for the child's actual mother.*

What's in a name? Plenty. By invariably referring to Mrs. Whitehead as a surrogate, the media, the courts and, unwittingly, Mrs. Whitehead herself tacitly validated the point of view of the Sterns, who naturally wanted to render Mrs. Whitehead's role in producing Baby M as notional as possible,

---

* In this article I will use the terms "contract mother," "maternity contract" and their variants, except where I am indirectly quoting others.

the trivial physical means by which their desire—which is what really mattered—was fulfilled. And if Mrs. Whitehead was the substitute, then Dr. Stern must be the real thing.

Oddly enough, Mr. Stern, whose paternity consisted of ejaculating into a jar, was always referred to as the father or natural father or, rarely, biological father of Baby M, except by Mrs. Whitehead, who called him "the sperm donor." Although that is a far more accurate term for him than "surrogate mother" is for her (let alone "surrogate uterus," which is how the distinguished child psychologist Lee Salk referred to her), her use of it was widely taken as yet another proof of her irrational and cruel nature. Why was this harpy persecuting this nice man?

Surrogacy is a startling new technological development. This claim is a favorite of columnists and other instant experts, who, having solemnly warned that reproductive science is outstripping society's ability to deal with it, helplessly throw up their hands because—what can you do?—progress marches on. But a maternity contract is not a scientific development; it is a piece of paper. Physically, as Mary Beth Whitehead pointed out, it involves merely artificial insemination, a centuries-old technique which requires a device no more complicated than a turkey baster. And artificial insemination itself is a social contrivance, the purpose of which is to avert not infertility but infidelity.

What is new about contract motherhood lies in the realm of law and social custom. It is a means by which women sign away rights that, until the twentieth century, they rarely had: the right to legal custody of their children, and the right not to be bought, sold, lent, rented or given away. Throughout most of Western history and in many countries even today, there has been no need for such contracts because the law favored the father's claim to the child, sometimes even if the child was illegitimate (unless the child's mother was married, in which case her husband could claim the child). If a father chose to exercise his right of custody, the mother was in a weak position. In most societies, furthermore, a man in William Stern's situation could have legally or semilegally acquired another female whose child, as per above, would be legally his: a second (or third or tenth) wife, a concubine, a slave, a kept woman. This is the happy state of affairs to which the maternity contract seeks to return its signers.

Those who comb history, literature and the Bible for reassuring precedents ignore the social context of oppression in which those odd little tales unfold. Yes, Sarah suggested that Abraham impregnate Hagar in order "that I may obtain children by her," but Hagar was a slave. What's modern about the story is that Hagar, like Mary Beth Whitehead, seemed to think that her child was hers no matter what anyone said. The outcome of that ancient domestic experiment was, in any case, disastrous, especially for Baby Ishmael. So perhaps the Bible was trying to tell us something about what happens when people treat people like things.

Surrogacy is the answer to female infertility. It has widely and properly been noted that only the well-to-do can afford to contract for a baby. (The Sterns, with a combined income of more than $90,000, paid $25,000 all told for Baby M, with $10,000 going to Mrs. Whitehead.) Less often has it been remarked that contract maternity is not a way for infertile women to get children, although the mothers often speak as though it were. It is a way for men to get children. Elizabeth Stern's name does not even appear on the contract, the legality of whch depends on it being an agreement between two biological parents. Had Mr. Stern filed for divorce before Baby M was born, had he died or become non compos, Dr. Stern would have been out of luck. Even after she became Baby M's primary caretaker, until the adoption went through, she had no more claim on the child than a baby-sitter. Rather than empower infertile women through an act of sisterly generosity, maternity contracts make one woman a baby machine and the other irrelevant.

And there is no reason to assume that contracts will be limited to men married to infertile women—indeed, the Sterns have already broken that barrier—or even to men married at all. I can hear the precedent-setting argument already: Why, your honor, should a man's drive to procreate, his constitutional right to the joys of paternity, be dependent on the permission of a woman? No doubt, this further innovation will be presented as a gesture of female altruism, too ("I just wanted to give him the One Thing a man can't give himself"). But take away the mothers' delusion that they are making babies for other women, and what you have left is what, in cold, hard fact, we already have: the limited-use purchase of women's bodies by men—reproductive prostitution.

So what? A woman has the right to control her body. The issue in contract motherhood is not whether a woman can bear a child for whatever reason she likes but whether she can be legally bound to a promise to sell that child—a whole other person, not an aspect of her body—to its father. Judge Sorkow is surely the only person on earth who thinks William Stern paid Mary Beth Whitehead $10,000 merely to conceive and carry a baby and not also to transfer that baby to him.

Actually, maternity contracts have the potential to do great harm to the cause of women's physical autonomy. Right now a man cannot legally control the conduct of a woman pregnant by him. He cannot force her to have an abortion or not have one, to manage her pregnancy and delivery as he thinks best, or to submit to fetal surgery or a cesarean. Nor can he sue her if, through what he considers to be negligence, she miscarries or produces a defective baby. A maternity contract could give a man all those powers, except, possibly, the power to compel abortion, the only clause in the Stern-Whitehead contract that Judge Sorkow found invalid. Mr. Stern, for instance, seemed to think he had the right to tell Mrs. Whitehead's doctors what drugs to give her during labor. We've already had the spectacle of policemen forcibly removing five-month-old Baby M from the arms of Mrs. Whitehead, the only mother she knew (so much for the best interests of the child!). What's next? State troopers guarding contract mothers to make sure they drink their milk?

Even if no money changed hands, the right-to-control-your-body argument would be unpersuasive. After all, the law already limits your right to do what you please with your body: You can't throw it off the Brooklyn Bridge, or feed it Laetrile, or even drive it around many places without a seat belt. But money does change hands, and everybody, male and female, needs to be protected by law from the power of money to coerce or entice people to do things that seriously compromise their basic and most intimate rights, such as the right to health or life. You can sell your blood, but you can't sell your kidney. In fact, you can't even donate your kidney except under the most limited circumstances, no matter how fiercely you believe that this is the way you were meant to serve your fellow man and no matter how healthy you are. The risk of coercion is simply too great, and your kidney just too irreplaceable.

Supporters of contract motherhood talk about having a baby for pay as if it were like selling blood, or sperm, or breast milk. It is much more like selling a vital organ. Unlike a man, who produces billions of sperm and can theoretically father thousands of children at zero physical risk to himself, a woman can bear only a small number of children, and the physical cost to her can be as high as death. She cannot know in advance what a given pregnancy will mean for her health or for her ability to bear more children. (Interestingly, both the Sterns, who delayed parenthood until they found pregnancy too risky, and the Whiteheads, who foreclosed having more children with Mr. Whitehead's vasectomy, show just how unpredictable extrapolations from one's reproductive present are as guides to the future.) How can it be acceptable to pay a woman to risk her life, health and fertility so that a man can have his own biological child, yet morally heinous to pay healthy people to sacrifice "extra" organs to achieve the incomparably greater aim of saving a life? We're scandalized when we read of Asian sterilization campaigns in which men are paid to be vasectomized—and not just because of the abuses to which those campaigns are notoriously subject but because they seem, by their very nature, to take advantage of people's shortsightedness in order to deprive them forever of something precious. Why is hiring women to have babies and give them away any better?

The question of payment is critical because although contract mothers prefer to tell the television cameras about their longing to help humanity, studies have shown that almost nine out of ten wouldn't help humanity for free. (Well, it's a job. Would you do your job for free?) But women to whom $10,000 is a significant amount of money are the ones who live closest to the economic edge and have the fewest alternative ways of boosting their income in a crisis. Right now contract motherhood is still considered a rather outré thing to do, and women often have to talk their families into it. But if it becomes a socially acceptable way for a wife to help out the family budget, how can the law protect women from being coerced into contracts by their husbands? Or their relatives? Or their creditors? It can't. In fact, it can't guarantee uncoerced consent even when no money changes hands. *The New York Times* has already discovered a case in which a family matriarch successfully pressured one relative to produce a child for another.

If contract motherhood takes hold, a woman's "right to control her body" by selling her pregnancies will become the modern equivalent of "she's sitting on a fortune." Her husband's unpaid debts, her children's unfixed teeth, the cramped apartment and the junky car, will all be her fault, the outcome of her selfish refusal to sell what nature gave her.

A deal's a deal. This is what it's really all about, isn't it? To hear the chorus of hosannas currently being raised to this sacred tenet of market economics, you'd think the entire structure of law and morality would collapse about our ears if one high-school-dropout housewife in New Jersey was allowed to keep her baby. "One expects a prostitute to fulfill a contract," intoned Lawrence Stone, the celebrated Princeton University historian, in *The New York Times.* (Should the poor girl fail to show up at her regular time, the campus police are presumably to tie her up and deliver her into one's bed.) Some women argue that to allow Mrs. Whitehead to back out of her pledge would stigmatize all women as irrational and incapable of adulthood under the law. You'd think she had signed a contract to trade sowbellies at $5 and then gave premenstrual syndrome as her reason for canceling.

But is a deal a deal? Not always. Not, for instance, when it involves something illegal: prostitution (sorry, Professor Stone), smuggling, slavery, polygyny, sweatshop labor, division of stolen goods and, oh yes, baby selling. Nor does it matter how voluntary such a contract is. So if your ambition in life is to be an indentured servant or a co-wife, you will have to fulfill this desire in a country where what Michael Kinsley calls "the moral logic of capitalism" has advanced so far that the untrained eye might mistake it for the sort of patriarchal semifeudalism practiced in provincial Iran.

Well, you say, suppose we decided that contract motherhood wasn't prostitution or baby selling but some other, not flatly illegal, transaction: sale of parental rights to the father or some such. Then a deal would be a deal, right? Wrong. As anyone who has ever shopped for a co-op apartment in New York City knows, in the world of commerce, legal agreements are abrogated, modified, renegotiated and bought out all the time. What happens when contracts are not fulfilled is what most of contract law is about.

Consider the comparatively civilized world of publishing. A writer signs up with one publisher, gets a better offer from another, pays back his advance—maybe—and moves on. Or a writer signs up to produce a novel but finds she'd rather die than see it printed, although her editor thinks it's a surefire best-seller. Does the publisher forcibly take possession of the manuscript and print 100,000 copies because it's his property and a deal's a deal? No. The writer gives back the advance or submits another idea or persuades her editor she's such a genius she ought to be given even more money to write a really good book. And, somehow, Western civilization continues.

The closer we get to the murky realm of human intimacy the more reluctant we are to enforce contracts in anything like their potential severity. Marriage, after all, is a contract. Yet we permit divorce. Child-support agreements are contracts. Yet a woman cannot bar the father of her children from leaving investment banking for the less lucrative profession of subway musician. Engagement is, if not usually a formal contract, a public pledge of great seriousness. Yet the bride or groom abandoned at the altar has not been able to file a breach of promise suit for generations. What have we learned since desperate spouses lit out for the territory and jilted maidens jammed the courts? That in areas of profound human feeling, you cannot promise because you cannot know, and pretending otherwise would result in far more misery than allowing people to cut their losses.

When Mary Beth Whitehead signed her contract, she was promising something it is not in anyone's power to promise: not to fall in love with her baby. To say, as some do, that she "should have known" because she'd had two children already is like saying a man should have known how he'd feel about his third wife because he'd already been married twice before. Why should mothers be held to a higher standard of self-knowledge than spouses? Or, more to the point, than fathers? In a recent California case, a man who provided a woman friend with sperm, no strings attached, changed his mind when the child was born and sued for visitation rights. He won. Curiously, no one has suggested that the decision stigmatized all males as hyperemotional dirty-dealers.

Fatherhood and motherhood are identical. It is at this point that one begins to feel people have resigned their common sense entirely. True, a man and a woman contribute equally to the genetic makeup of a baby. But twenty-three pairs of chromosomes do not a baby make. In the usual course of events the woman is then pregnant for nine months and goes through childbirth, a detail overlooked by those who compare maternity contracts to sperm donation. The proper parallel to sperm donation is egg donation.

Feminists who argue that respecting Mrs. Whitehead's maternal feelings will make women prisoners of the "biology is destiny" arguments should think again. The Baby M decision did not disclaim the power of biology at all; it exalted male biology at the expense of female. Judge Sorkow paid tribute to Mr. Stern's drive to procreate; it was only Mrs. Whitehead's longing to nurture that he scorned. That Baby M had Mr. Stern's genes was judged a fact of supreme importance—more important than Mrs. Whitehead's genes, pregnancy and child-birth put together. We might as well be back in the days when a woman was seen merely as a kind of human potting soil for a man's seed.

Speaking as a pregnant person, I find the view of maternity inherent in maternity contracts profoundly demeaning. Pregnancy and delivery are not "services" performed for the baby's father. The unborn child is not riding about inside a woman like a passenger in a car. A pregnant woman is not, as one contract mother put it, "a human incubator"; she is engaged in a constructive task, in taxing physical work. Some of this work is automatic, and no less deserving of respect for that, but much of it is not—an increasing amount, it would appear, to judge by doctors' ever-lengthening list of dos and don'ts.

Now, why do I follow my doctor's advice: swill milk, take vitamins, eschew alcohol, cigarettes, caffeine, dental X-rays and even the innocent aspirin? And why, if I had to, would I do a lot more to help my baby to be born healthy, including things that are uncomfortable and wearisome (like staying in bed for months, as a friend of mine had to) or even detrimental to my own body (like fetal surgery)? It's not because I want to turn out a top-of-the-line product, or feel a sense of duty to the baby's dad, or have invested the baby with the rights and privileges of an American citizen whose address just happens to be my uterus. I do it because I love the baby. Even before it's born, I'm already forming a relationship with it. You can call that biology or social conditioning or an emotional fantasy. Perhaps, like romantic love, it is all three at once. But it's part of what pregnancy is—just ask the millions of pregnant women who feel this way, often to their own astonishment, sometimes under much less auspicious circumstances than Mrs. Whitehead's. It makes my blood boil when it is suggested that if contract mothers delivered under anesthesia and never saw their babies they wouldn't get a chance to "bond" and would feel no loss. I suppose the doctor could just tell them that they gave birth to a watermelon.

And so we arrive at the central emotional paradox of the Baby M case. We accept the notion that a man can have intense fatherly emotion for a child he's never seen, whose mother he's never slept with, let alone rubbed her back, or put his hand on her belly to feel the baby kick, or even taken her to the hospital. But a woman who violates her promise and loves the child she's had inside her for nine months, risked her health for, given birth to . . . She must be some kind of nut.

Women need more options, not fewer. To suggest that female poverty can be ameliorated by poor mothers selling their children to wealthy fathers is a rather Swiftian concept. But why stop at contract motherhood when there's still a flourishing market for adoptive babies? Let enterprising poor women take up childbearing as a cottage industry and conceive expressly for the purpose of selling the baby to the highest bidder. And since the law permits parents to give up older children for adoption, why shouldn't they be allowed to sell them as well? Ever on the reproductive forefront, New Jersey recently gave the world the sensational case of a father who tried to sell his four-year-old daughter to her dead mother's relatives for $100,000. Why he was arrested for attempting what Mary Beth Whitehead was forced to do is anybody's guess.

Even leaving aside the fact that maternity contracts involve the sale of a human being, do women need another incredibly low-paying service job that could damage their health and possibly even kill them, that opens up the most private areas of life to interference by a pair of total strangers, that they cannot get unless they first sign an ironclad contract forgoing a panoply of elementary human rights? By that logic, working in a sweatshop is an option, too—which is exactly what sweatshop employers have always maintained.

But people are going to do it anyway. Shouldn't they be protected? There are some troubling practices (drinking, smoking, infidelity) so entrenched in mass behavior and regarded as acceptable by so many that to make them illegal would be both undemocratic and futile. Contract motherhood is not one of them. In ten years only about 500 women have signed up. So the argument that we should legitimize it because it's just human nature in its infinite variety is not valid—yet.

Now, it's probably true that some women will bear children for money no matter what the law says. In the privacy of domestic life all sorts of strange arrangements are made. But why should the state enforce such bargains? Feminists who think that regulation would protect the mother miss the whole point of the maternity contract, which is precisely to deprive her of protections she would have if she had signed nothing. If the contracts were unenforceable, the risk would be where it belongs, on the biological father and his wife, whose disappointment if the mother reneges, though real, can hardly be compared with a mother's unwilling loss of her just-born child. The real loser, of course, would be the baby-broker. (Noel Keane, the lawyer who arranged for Baby M, says he made about $300,000 last year in fees for such services.) And that would be a very good thing.

But most surrogates have been pleased with their experience. Perhaps the Baby M trial is just a hard case making a bad law. It's possible to be horrified by what happened to Mary Beth Whitehead and still think that contract motherhood can be a positive thing if carefully regulated. If there had been better screening at the clinic, if the contract had included a grace period, if actual infertility had been required of Elizabeth Stern, we would never have heard of Baby M. If, if, if.

Regulation might make contract motherhood less haphazard, but there is no way it can be made anything other than what it is: an inherently unequal relationship involving the sale of a woman's body and a child. The baby-broker's client is the father; his need is the one being satisfied; he pays the broker's fee. No matter how it is regulated, the business will have to reflect that priority. That's why the bill being considered in New York State specifically denies the mother a chance to change her mind, although the stringency of the Stern-Whitehead contract in this regard was the one thing pundits assured the public would not happen again. Better screening procedures would simply mean more accurately weeding out the troublemakers and selecting for docility, naïveté, low self-esteem and lack of money for legal fees. Free psychological counseling for the mothers, touted by some brokers as evidence of their care and concern, would merely be manipulation by another name. True therapy seeks to increase a person's sense of self, not reconcile one to being treated as an instrument.

Even if the business could be managed so that all the adults involved were invariably pleased with the outcome, it would still be wrong, because they are not the only people involved. There are, for instance, the mother's other children. Prospective contract mothers, Mrs. Whitehead included, do not seem to consider for two seconds the message they are sending to their kids. But how can it not damage a child to watch Mom cheerfully produce and sell its half-sibling while Dad stands idly by? I'd love to be a fly on the wall as a mother reassures her kids that of course she loves them no matter what they do; it's just their baby sister who had a price tag.

And, of course, there is the contract baby. To be sure, there are worse ways of coming into the world, but not many, and none that are elaborately prearranged by sane people.

Much is made of the so-called trauma of adoption, but adoption is a piece of cake compared with contracting. Adoptive parents can tell their child, Your mother loved you so much that she gave you up, even though it made her sad, because that was best for you. What can the father and adoptive mother of a contract baby say? Your mother needed $10,000? Your mother wanted to do something nice for us, so she made you? The Sterns can't even say that. They'll have to make do with something like, Your mother loved you so much she wanted to keep you, but we took you anyway, because a deal's a deal, and anyway, she was a terrible person. Great.

Oh, lighten up. Surrogacy fills a need. There's a shortage of babies for adoption, and people have the right to a child. What is the need contract motherhood fills? It is not the need for a child, exactly. That need is met by adoption—although not very well, it's true, especially if prospective parents have their hearts set on a "perfect baby," a healthy white newborn. The so-called baby shortage is really a shortage of these infants. (Shortage from the would-be adoptive parents' point of view; from the point of view of the birth mothers or Planned Parenthood, there's still a baby surplus.) What William Stern wanted, however, was not just a perfect baby; the Sterns did not, in fact, seriously investigate adoption. He wanted a perfect baby with his genes and a medically vetted mother who would get out of his life forever immediately after giving birth. That's a tall order, and one no other class of father—natural, step-, adoptive—even claims to be entitled to. Why should the law bend itself into a pretzel to gratify it?

The Vatican's recent document condemning all forms of conception but marital intercourse was marked by the church's usual political arrogance and cheeseparing approach to sexual intimacy, but it was right about one thing: You don't have a right to a child, any more than you have a right to a spouse. You only have the right to try to have one. Goods can be distributed according to ability to pay or not. People shouldn't be.

It's really that simple.

1987

On the Merits

The other day my old classmate Allen and I were discussing who would be the next editor in chief of the influential magazine whose staff he had recently joined. I proposed Rosemary, the deputy editor: She had seniority, she was extremely able, she was practically doing the job already. Allen looked at me as if I had suggested sending out a spacecraft for the editor of *The Neptune Gazette*. Come on, he said, you know they'd never give it to a woman. So who do you think it will be? I asked innocently. Well, he replied with a modest blush, actually, me.

This exchange made me think again about one of the more insidious arguments being made in the current onslaught against affirmative action: Advancing women and minorities on the basis of sex and race damages their self-esteem. According to Clarence M. Pendleton, Jr., Reagan-appointed chairman of the United States Commission on Civil Rights, those who benefit from social and legal pressures on their behalf know in their hearts that they are unworthy and suffer terribly because they fear, correctly, that they won't measure up. Worse, the women and minorities who would have won the golden prizes anyway—the college acceptance, the job, the promotion—are guilty by association: Everyone thinks they're tokens, even if they're not.

It's an ingenious argument, because it not only appears to demonstrate concern for the same constituency as affirmative action but also makes affirmative action seem by comparison both crude and condescending. What is money, after all, or a job title, compared with the priceless gift of psychological peace? Don't we all need to think we are rewarded on our merits? Yes, indeed, which is why I'm very worried about my friend Allen's peace of mind. If his publisher promotes him over Rosemary because he is a man, won't Allen spend a lot of sleepless nights wondering if the world is snickering at him behind his back?

Not on your life. Allen has been blithely ignoring such threats to his self-esteem for decades.

We both attended Harvard-Radcliffe, for example, at a time when the ratio of male to female students was fixed at five to one. Granted that the pool of female applicants was smaller, the fact remains it was harder for girls to get in. Everyone knew this, but Allen and his friends never saw themselves as having been rounded up to fill an inflated male quota. Nor did they see as tarnished victories their acceptance into the many all-male clubs and activities that flourished in those benighted years—the Signet Society, for instance, where literary Harvard men were served lunch by literary Radcliffe women employed as waitresses—or scorn to go off to Europe on postgraduate fellowships closed to female classmates.

If the self-esteem argument were true, who would get a good night's sleep? After all, we live in a society where all sorts of considerations besides merit are accepted as valid means of choosing candidates. Because elite schools want diversity, it's easier for a student from Montana to get in than one from New York City. Because lawmakers want to reward military service, veterans get lifelong preference for a slew of state and federal jobs. Because political parties want votes, they craft ethnically and geographically balanced tickets.

Some of these nonmerit considerations are rather shady, to say the least. At the Ivy League college where I taught last year, a delicious scandal came to light when an alumnus wrote an outraged letter to the campus newspaper alleging that his son had been passed over for admission in the rush to accept women and blacks. It turned out that although the overall odds of acceptance were one in seven, for the children of alumni they were almost one in two. Many sheepish things were said in defense of this practice: For example, administrators cited the natural desire of the college to create a sense of continuity between the generations, translated by campus cynics as the natural desire of the college to receive large financial contributions from prosperous grads. But I'm still waiting for Mr. Pendleton to acknowledge the existence of alumni-child preferences, let alone express solicitude for the self-esteem of alumni children.

It's a curious thing. As long as we're talking about white men competing with each other, we tacitly acknowledge that we live in a realistic world of a Balzac novel, a world in which we know perfectly well that Harvard C's beat A's from Brooklyn College, in which family connections and a good tennis serve never hurt, and sycophancy, backstabbing and organizational inertia carry the undeserving into top jobs every day of the week. Add women and blacks into the picture, though, and suddenly the scene shifts. Now we're in Plato's Republic, where sternly impartial philosopher-kings award laurels to the deserving after nights of fasting and prayer. Or did, before affirmative action threw its spanner into the meritocratic works.

So how do the beneficiaries of social privilege avoid the dreaded inferiority complex? That's where individual psychology and social myopia come in. On the personal level they live in both worlds at once: *I* slave away in Plato's Republic, while *you* weasel your way down the boulevards of Balzac's Paris. This collective delusion is so culturally approved that people who get the formula backward are considered to be victims of "the impostor syndrome" and in need of psychiatric help.

To transform America into a true meritocracy would be a fascinating experiment in social engineering, but it would make the minor adjustments required by affirmative action look like piano tuning. We'd have to strip the credentials of all male doctors over the age of thirty-five, for instance, since they got into medical school back when a woman had to be Albert Schweitzer in skirts to win a place in the class. Ditto for lawyers, engineers, tenured professors, corporate executives and military officers. The children of the famous would have to change their names. Perhaps it would be too cruel to force the powerful to remain celibate in order to discourage nepotism. But we could certainly make it a criminal offense to marry the boss's daughter, or even to take her out for coffee.

Brave New World or simple justice? Whichever, I'm ready for it, whenever Mr. Pendleton gives the word; even though, as an alumni child, I'll have to turn in my college diploma. Because in the perfect meritocracy that would result, Rosemary would get that job. And Allen? Well, he'd have something even more precious. His self-esteem.

1985

Naming and Blaming: Media Goes Wilding in Palm Beach

I drink, I swear, I flirt, I tell dirty jokes. I have also, at various times, watched pornographic videos, had premarital sex, hitchhiked, and sunbathed topless in violation of local ordinances. True, I don't have any speeding tickets, but I don't have a driver's license either. Perhaps I'm subconsciously afraid of my "drives"? There are other things, too, and if I should ever bring rape charges against a rich, famous, powerful politician's relative, *The New York Times* will probably tell you all about them—along with, perhaps, my name. Suitably adorned with anonymous quotes, these revelations will enable you, the public, to form your own opinion: Was I asking for trouble, or did I just make the whole thing up?

In April the media free-for-all surrounding the alleged rape of a Palm Beach woman by William Kennedy Smith, Senator Ted Kennedy's nephew, took a vicious turn as the *Times*—following NBC, following the *Globe* (supermarket, not Boston, edition), following a British scandal sheet, following *another*

British scandal sheet—went public with the woman's name, and a lot more: her traffic violations, her mediocre high school grades, her "little wild streak," her single motherhood, her mother's divorce and upwardly mobile remarriage. Pretty small potatoes, really; she sounds like half my high school classmates. But it did make a picture: bad girl, loose woman, floozy.

Or did it? In a meeting with more than 300 outraged staff members, national editor Soma Golden said that the *Times* could not be held responsible for "every weird mind that reads [the paper]." NBC News chief Michael Gartner was more direct: "Who she is is material in this. . . . You try to give viewers as many facts as you can and let them make up their minds." Forget that almost none of these "facts" will be admissible in court, where a jury will nonetheless be expected to render a verdict.

In the ensuing furor, just about every advocate for rape victims has spoken out in favor of preserving the long-standing media custom of anonymity, and in large part the public seems to agree. But the media,* acting in its capacity as the guardian of public interest, has decided that naming the victim is an issue up for grabs. And so we are having one of those endless, muddled, two-sides-to-every-question debates that, by ignoring as many facts as possible and by weighing all arguments equally, gives us that warm American feeling that truth must lie somewhere in the middle. Anna Quindlen, meet Alan Dershowitz. Thank you very much, but our time is just about up.

Sometimes, of course, the truth does lie somewhere in the

---

* I use "media" in the singular (rather than the strictly grammatical plural) because I am talking about the communications industry as a social institution that, while hardly monolithic (as the debate over naming shows), transcends the different means—"media" plural—by which the news is conveyed.

middle. But not this time. There is no good reason to publish the names of rape complainants without their consent, and many compelling reasons not to. The arguments advanced in favor of publicity reveal fundamental misconceptions about both the nature of the media and the nature of rape.

Let's take a look at what proponents of naming are saying.

The media has a duty to report what it knows. Where have you been? The media keeps information secret all the time. Sometimes it does so on the ground of "taste," a waffle-word that means whatever an editorial board wants it to mean. Thus, we hear about (some of) the sexual high jinks of heterosexual celebrities but not about those of socially equivalent closet-dwellers, whose opposite-sex escorts are portrayed, with knowing untruthfulness, as genuine romantic interests. We are spared—or deprived of, depending on your point of view—the gruesome and salacious details of many murders. (Of all the New York dailies, only *Newsday* reported that notorious Wall Street wife-killer Joseph Pikul was wearing women's underwear when arrested. Not fit to print? I was *riveted*.) Sometimes the media fudges the truth to protect third parties from embarrassment, which is why the obituaries would have us believe that eminent young bachelors are dying in large numbers only from pneumonia.

And of course sometimes the media censors itself in "the national interest." The claim that the media constitutes a fourth estate, a permanent watchdog, if not outright adversary, of the government, has always been a self-serving myth. Watergate occurred almost twenty years ago and has functioned ever since as a kind of sentimental talisman, like Charles Foster Kane's Rosebud sled. As we saw during the Gulf War, the media can live, when it chooses, quite comfortably with government-imposed restrictions. Neither NBC nor *The New York Times*, so quick to supply their audiences with the inside scoop on the Palm Beach woman, felt any such urgency about Operation Desert Storm.

Anonymous charges are contrary to the American way. Anonymous charges are contrary to American *jurisprudence*. The Palm Beach woman has not made an anonymous accusation. Her name is known to the accused and his attorney, and if the case comes to trial, she will have to appear publicly in court, confront the defendant, give testimony and be cross-examined. But the media is not a court, as the many lawyers who have made this argument—most prominently Alan Dershowitz and Isabelle Pinzler of the American Civil Liberties Union's Women's Rights Project—ought to know.

The media itself argues in favor of anonymity when that serves its own purposes. Reporters go to jail rather than reveal their sources, even when secrecy means protecting a dangerous criminal, impeding the process of justice or denying a public figure the ability to confront his or her accusers. People wouldn't talk to reporters, the press claims, if their privacy couldn't be guaranteed—the same greater-social-good argument it finds unpersuasive when made about rape victims and their reluctance to talk, unprotected, to the police. The media's selective interest in concealment, moreover, undermines its vaunted mission on behalf of the public's right to know. Might not the identity of an anonymous informant (one of those "sources close to the White House" or "highly placed observers," for instance) help the public "make up its mind" about the reliability of the statements? I don't want to digress here into the complex issue of protecting sources, but there can be little question that the practice allows powerful people, in and out of government, to manipulate information for their own ends. Interestingly, the *Times* story on the Palm Beach woman concealed (thirteen times!) the names of those spreading malicious gossip about her, despite the *Times*'s own custom of not using anonymous pejoratives. That custom was resuscitated in time for the paper's circumspect profile of William Smith, which did not detail the accusations against him of prior acquaintance rapes that have been published by *The National Enquirer* and the gossip columnist Taki, and which referred only vaguely to "rumors" of "a pattern of aggressiveness toward women in private." (These, the *Times* said, it could not confirm—unlike the accuser's "little wild streak.")

How *did* the *Times* manage to amass such a wealth of dirt about the Palm Beach woman so quickly? It's hard to picture the reporter, distinguished China hand Fox Butterfield, peeking into the window of her house to see what books were on her toddler's shelf. Could some of his information or some of his leads have come, directly or circuitously, from the detectives hired by the Kennedy family to investigate the woman and her friends—detectives who, let's not forget, have been the subject of complaints of witness intimidation? The *Times* denies it, but rumors persist. One could argue that, in this particular case, *how* the *Times* got the story was indeed part of the story—perhaps the most important part.

That anonymity is held to be essential to the public good in a wide variety of cases but is damned as a form of censorship in the Palm Beach case shows that what the media is concerned with is not the free flow of information *or* the public good. What is at stake is the media's status, power and ability to define and control information in accordance with the views of those who run the media.

Consider, for example, the case of men convicted of soliciting prostitutes. Except for the occasional athlete, such men receive virtual anonymity in the press. Remember the flap in 1979 when Manhattan D.A. Robert Morgenthau released a list of recently convicted johns and the *Daily News* and two local radio stations went public with it? Universal outrage! Never mind that solicitation is a crime, that convictions are a matter of public record, that the wives and girlfriends of these men might find knowledge of this record extremely useful, and that (rightly or wrongly) society has declared its interest in deterring prostitution. Publicizing the names of johns, opponents argued, was vindictive, subjected ordinary people to the glaring light of publicity for a peccadillo, could destroy the men's marriages and reputations, and stigmatized otherwise decent people. The lists were discontinued. Privacy for johns, however, has never meant privacy for women accused of prostitution, whose names are published all the time, regardless of the personal consequences. Thus with prostitution, a two-person crime, hallowed journalistic practice treats the privacy claims of the perpetrators quite differently. But with rape, if the proponents of naming have their way, the rapist and his victim are to be treated the same, even though rape is a one-person crime. Shouldn't rape victims get at least as much forbearance from the press as the men listed in the Mayflower Madam's black book?

But here the woman's identity was already widely known. Well, I didn't know it. I did, however, know the name of the Central Park jogger—like virtually every other journalist in the country, the entire readership of *The Amsterdam News* (50,000) and the listening audience of WLIB radio (45,000). Anna Quindlen, in her courageous column dissenting from the *Times*'s profile naming the Palm Beach woman, speculated that roughly equivalent large numbers of people knew the identity of the jogger as knew that of William Smith's alleged victim before NBC and the *Times* got into the act. Yet the media went to extraordinary lengths to protect the remaining shreds of the jogger's privacy—film clips were blipped, quotes censored.

What separates the jogger from the Palm Beach woman? You don't have to be the Reverend Al Sharpton to suspect that protecting the jogger's identity was more than a chivalrous gesture. Remember that she, too, was originally blamed for her assault: What was she doing in the park so late? Who did she think she was? It's all feminism's fault for deluding women into thinking that their safety could, or should, be everywhere guaranteed. But partly as a result of the severity of her injuries, the jogger quickly became the epitome of the innocent victim, the symbol, as Joan Didion pointed out in the *New York Review of Books*, for New York City itself (white, prosperous, plucky) endangered by the black underclass. A white Wellesley graduate with a Wall Street job attacked out of nowhere by a band of violent black strangers and, because of her comatose state, unable even to bring a rape complaint—this, to the media, is "real rape." The Palm Beach woman, on the other hand, is of working-class origins, a single mother, a frequenter of bars, who went voluntarily to her alleged attacker's house (as who, in our starstruck society, would not?). The jogger could have been the daughter of the men who kept her name out of the news. But William Kennedy Smith could have been their son.

Rape is like other crimes and should be treated like other crimes. Isn't that what you feminists are always saying? As the coverage of the Palm Beach case proves, rape isn't treated like other crimes. There is no other crime in which the character, behavior and past of the complainant are seen as central elements in determining whether a crime has occurred. There are lots of crimes that could not take place without carelessness, naïveté, ignorance or bad judgment on the part of the victims: mail fraud ("Make $100,000 at home in your spare time!"), confidence games and many violent crimes as well. But when my father was burglarized after forgetting to lock the cellar door, the police did not tell him he had been asking for it. And when an elderly lady (to cite Amy Pagnozzi's example in the *New York Post*) is defrauded of her life savings by a con artist, the con artist is just as much a thief as if he'd broken into his victim's safe-deposit box. "The complainant showed incredibly bad judgment, Your Honor," is not a legal defense.

Why is rape different? Because lots of people, too often including the ones in the jury box, think women really do want to be forced into sex, or by acting or dressing or drinking in a certain way give up the right to say no, or are the sort of people (i.e., not nuns) who gave up the right to say no to one man by saying yes to another, or are by nature scheming, irrational and crazy. Lots of people also think men cannot be expected to control themselves, are entitled to take by force what they cannot get by persuasion and are led on by women who because they are scheming, irrational and crazy, change their minds in mid-sex. My files bulge with stories that show how widespread these beliefs are: the Wisconsin judge who put a child molester on probation because he felt the three-year-old female victim had acted provocatively; the Florida jury that exonerated an accused rapist because his victim was wearing disco attire; and so on.

In a bizarre column defending Ted Kennedy's role on the night in question, William Safire took aim at the Palm Beach woman, who was "apparently" not "taught that drinking all night and going to a man's house at 3:30 a.m. places one in what used to be called an occasion of sin." (All her mother's fault, as usual.) The other woman present in the Kennedy mansion that night, a waitress named Michelle Cassone, has made herself a mini-celebrity by telling any reporter who will pay for her time that she, too, believes that women who drink and date, including herself, are "fair game."

By shifting the debate to the question of merely naming victims, the media preempts a discussion of the way it reports all crimes with a real or imaginary sexual component. But as the *Times* profile shows, naming cannot be divorced from blaming. When the victim is young and attractive (and in the tabloids *all* female victims are attractive), the sexual element in the crime is always made its central feature—even when, as in the case of Marla Hanson, the model who was slashed by hired thugs and whose character was savaged in *New York*, there is no sexual element. I mean no belittlement of rape to suggest it was one of the lesser outrages visited on the Central Park jogger. She was also beaten so severely she lost 75 percent of her blood and suffered permanent physical, neurological and cognitive damage. Yet, paradoxically, it was the rape that seized the imagination of the media, and that became the focus of the crime both for her defenders and for those who defended her attackers.

Naming rape victims will remove the stigma against rape. Of all the arguments in favor of naming victims, this is the silliest, and the most insincere. Sure, NBC's Michael Gartner told *Newsweek*, the consequences will be "extraordinarily difficult for this generation, but it may perhaps help their daughters and granddaughters." How selfish of women to balk at offering themselves on the altar of little girls yet unborn! If Gartner wishes to make a better world for my descendants, he is amply well placed to get cracking. He could demand nonsensationalized reporting of sex crimes; he could hire more female reporters and producers; he could use NBC News to dispel false notions about rape—for example, the idea that "who the woman is is material." Throughout the country there are dozens of speakouts against rape at which victims publicly tell of their experiences. Every year there are Take Back the Night marches in Manhattan. Where are the cameras and the reporters on these occasions? Adding misery to hundreds of thousands of women a year and—as just about every expert in the field believes—dramatically lowering the already abysmal incidence of rape reporting (one in ten) will not help my granddaughter; it will only make it more likely that her grandmother, her mother and she herself will be raped by men who have not been brought to justice.

This argument is, furthermore, based on a questionable assumption. Why would society blame rape victims less if it knew who they were? Perhaps its censure would be amplified. Instead of thinking, If ordinary, decent, conventional women get raped in large numbers it *can't* be their fault, people might well think, Goodness, there are a lot more women asking for it than we thought. After the invasion of Kuwait, in which scores of women were raped by Iraqi soldiers, there was no dispensation from the traditional harsh treatment of rape victims, some of whom, pregnant and in disgrace, had attempted suicide, gone into hiding or fled the country. One woman told *USA Today* that she wished she were dead. America is not Kuwait, but here, too, many believe that a woman can't be raped against her will and that damaged goods are damaged goods. (Curious how publicity is supposed to lessen the stigma against rape victims but only adds to the suffering of johns.)

One also has to wonder about the urgency with which Gartner and the other male proponents of the antistigma theory, with no history of public concern for women, declare themselves the best judge of women's interests and advocate a policy of which they themselves will never have to bear the consequences. Gartner cited, as did many others, the *Des Moines Register* profile of a named rape victim but neglected to mention that the victim, Nancy Ziegenmeyer, volunteered the use of her name, seven months after reporting the crime—in other words, after she had had a chance to come to terms with her experience and to inform her family and friends in a way she found suitable. (Ziegenmeyer, by the way, opposes involuntary naming.) Why is it that, where women are concerned, the difference between choice and coercion eludes so many? Rapists, too, persuade themselves that they know what women really want and need.

William Kennedy Smith's name has been dragged through the mud. Why should his accuser be protected? Actually, Smith has been portrayed rather favorably in the media. No anonymous pejoratives for him: He is "one of the least spoiled and least arrogant of the young Kennedys" (*Time*); an "unlikely villain" (*Newsweek*); "a man of gentleness and humor," "the un-Kennedy," "a good listener" (*The New York Times*); from a "wounded," "tragic" family (*passim*). Certainly he has been subjected to a great deal of unpleasant media attention, and even if he is eventually found innocent, some people will always suspect that he is guilty. But no one forced the media to sensationalize the story; that was a conscious editorial decision, not an act of God. Instead of heaping slurs on the Palm Beach woman in order to even things up, the media should be asking itself why it did not adopt a more circumspect attitude toward the case from the outset.

The tit-for-tat view of rape reporting appeals to many people because of its apparent impartiality. Feminists of the pure equal-treatment school like it because it looks gender neutral (as if rape were a gender-neutral crime). And nonfeminist men like it because, while looking gender neutral, it would, in practice, advantage men. "Should the press be in the business of protecting certain groups but not others—," wrote *Washington Post* columnist Richard Cohen, "alleged victims (females), but not the accused (males)? My answer is no." Cohen, like Michael Gartner, presents himself as having women's best interests at heart: "If rape's indelible stigma is ever to fade, the press has to stop being complicitous in perpetuating the sexist aura that surrounds it." Thus, by some mysterious alchemy, the media, which is perhaps the single biggest promoter of the sexist aura surrounding crimes of violence against women, can redeem itself by jettisoning the only policy it has that eases, rather than augments, the victim's anguish.

Behind the tit-for-tat argument lies a particular vision of rape in which the odds are even that the alleged victim is really the victimizer—a seductress, blackmailer, hysteric, who is bringing a false charge. That was the early word on the Palm Beach woman, and it's hard not to conclude that publicizing her identity was punitive: She's caused all this trouble, she's visiting yet more "tragedy" on America's royal family, and she'd better be telling the truth. In fact, the appeal of naming the victim seems to rest not in the hope that it "may perhaps" someday make rape reporting less painful but in the certainty that right now it makes such reporting *more* painful, thereby inhibiting false accusations. Although studies have repeatedly shown that fabricated rape charges are extremely rare, recent years have seen a number of cases: Tawana Brawley, for example, and Cathleen Crowell Webb, who recanted her testimony after finding Jesus and then hugged her newly freed no-longer-alleged assailant on the "Donahue" show. A year ago a Nebraska woman who admitted filing a false charge was ordered by a judge to purchase newspaper ads and radio spots apologizing to the man she had accused. (She was also sentenced to six months in jail.) It is not unknown for other criminal charges to be fabricated, but has anyone ever been forced into a public apology in those cases? The tenor of the equal-publicity argument is captured perfectly by the (female) letter writer to *Time* who suggested that newspapers publish both names and both photos, too. Why not bring back trial by ordeal and make the two of them grasp bars of red-hot iron?

Fundamentally, the arguments about naming rape victims center around two contested areas: acquaintance rape and privacy. While the women's movement has had some success in expanding the definition of rape to include sexual violation by persons known to the victim—as I write, *The New York Times* is running an excellent series on such rape, containing interviews with women named or anonymous by their choice (atonement?)—there is also a lot of backlash.

The all-male editorial board of the *New York Post*, which rather ostentatiously refused to print the Palm Beach woman's name, has actually proposed a change in the law to distinguish between "real rape" (what the jogger suffered) and acquaintance rape, confusedly described as a "sexual encounter, forced or not," that "has been preceded by a series of consensual activities." *Forced or not?*

At the other end of the literary social scale, there's Camille (No Means Yes) Paglia, academia's answer to Phyllis Schlafly, repackaging hoary myths about rape as a bold dissent from feminist orthodoxy and "political correctness." Indeed, an attack on the concept of acquaintance rape figures prominently in the many diatribes against current intellectual trends on campus. It's as though the notion of consensual sex were some incomprehensible French literary theory that threatened the very foundations of Western Civ. And, come to think of it, maybe it does.

Finally, there is the issue of privacy. Supporters of naming like to say that anonymity implies that rape is something to be ashamed of. But must this be its meaning? It says a great deal about the impoverishment of privacy as a value in our time that many intelligent people can find no justification for it but shame, guilt, cowardice and prudishness. As the tabloidization of the media proceeds apace, as the boundaries between the public and the personal waver and fade away, good citizenship has come to require of more and more people that they put themselves forward, regardless of the cost, as Exhibit A in a national civics lesson. In this sense, rape victims are in the same position as homosexuals threatened with "out-ing" for the good of other gays, or witnesses forced to give painful and embarrassing testimony in televised courtrooms so that the couch potatoes at home can appreciate the beauty of the legal process.

But there are lots of reasons a rape victim might not want her name in the paper that have nothing to do with shame. She might not want her mother to know, or her children, or her children's evil little classmates, or obscene phone callers, or other rapists. Every person reading this article probably has his or her secrets, things that aren't necessarily shameful but are liable to misconstructions, false sympathy and stupid questions from the tactless and ignorant. Things that are just plain nobody's business unless you want them to be.

Instead of denying privacy to rape victims, we should take a good hard look at our national passion for thrusting unwanted publicity on people who are not accused of wrongdoing but find themselves willy-nilly in the news. ("How did it *feel* to watch your child being torn to pieces by wild animals?" "It felt terrible, Maury, terrible.") I've argued here that society's attitudes toward rape justify privacy for rape complainants, and that indeed those attitudes lurk behind the arguments for publicity. But something else lurks there as well: a desensitization to the lurid and prurient way in which the media exploits the sufferings of any ordinary person touched by a noteworthy crime or disaster. Most of the people who have spoken out against anonymity are journalists, celebrity lawyers, media executives and politicos—people who put themselves forward in the press and on television as a matter of course and who are used to taking their knocks as the price of national attention. It must be hard for such people to sympathize with someone who doesn't want to play the media game—especially if it's in a "good cause."

I'm not at all sure there is a good cause here. Titillation, not education, seems the likely reason for the glare on the

Palm Beach case. But even if I'm unduly cynical and the media sincerely wishes to conduct a teach-in on rape, the interests of the public can be served without humiliating the complainant. Doctors educate one another with case histories in which patients are identified only by initials and in which other non-relevant identifying details are changed. Lawyers file briefs on behalf of Jane Doe and John Roe and expect the Supreme Court to "make up its mind" nonetheless.

If the media wants to educate the public about rape, it can do so without names. What the coverage of the Palm Beach case shows is that it needs to educate itself first.

1991

Checkbook Maternity:
When Is a Mother Not a Mother?

To the small and curious class of English words that have double and contradictory meanings—"moot," for example, and "cleave"—the word "mother" can now be added. Within the space of a single dazzling week this fall, this hoary old noun was redefined so thoroughly, in such mutually exclusive ways, that what it means now depends on which edition of the newspaper you read.

On October 23, in Orange County, California, Superior Court Judge Richard Parslow decided that the rightful mother of Baby Boy Johnson was not Anna Johnson, the black "gestational surrogate" who, for $10,000, carried him and birthed him, but Crispina Calvert, the wombless Asian-born woman who provided the egg from which, after in vitro fertilization with her (white) husband's sperm and implantation in Ms. Johnson, the baby grew. Declining, he said, to play Solomon and put the baby in the "crazy-making" position of having "two mothers"—or to follow California law, which defines the

mother as the woman who gives birth to the child—Judge
Parslow ruled that genes make the mom, as they do the dad.
Anna Johnson was merely a kind of foster mother, a "home,"
an "environment."

One wonders what Judge Parslow would make of a head-
line two days later. "Menopause Is Found No Bar to Pregnancy" announced *The New York Times*, reporting that doctors
had succeeded in making six prematurely menopausal women
pregnant by implanting each with donated eggs fertilized in
vitro with her husband's sperm. By Judge Parslow's reasoning,
of course, those women are merely foster mothers, homes and
environments, but so far no one has suggested this, much less
called for a reevaluation of Johnson's claim in the light of new
information about the value women place on pregnancy and
childbirth and the persistent (if apparently erroneous) belief
that the resultant babies belong to them.

To their credit, commentators have not regarded these
developments with unalloyed rapture. Perhaps they learned
something from the Baby M fracas. In that dispute, you will
remember, many intelligent people persuaded themselves that
the baby's rightful mother was a woman who had *no* biological
connection to it, and that its real mother, Mary Beth Whitehead, was a grasping madwoman because she did not think
she was, as child psychologist Lee Salk put it, a "surrogate
uterus." The New Jersey Supreme Court disagreed, restored
Whitehead's parental rights, which the lower court had abrogated, and, lo and behold, none of the confidently predicted
dire consequences ensued. Women are not regarded as too
emotional to make binding contracts, as some feminists feared,
nor has motherhood been more deeply consigned to the realm
of instinct and mystification. The child, now a toddler, has
not been destroyed or corrupted by contact with her mother:
Mary Beth Whitehead, the supposed Medea of the Mead-
owlands, turns out to be such a good mom, in fact, that *New*

York Times columnist Anna Quindlen, who observed one of the child's visits, felt moved to renounce her earlier anti-Whitehead position. Indeed, the only consequences have been positive: The child knows both her parents; paid Baby M–style arrangements have been outlawed in two states, the contracts declared unenforceable in three; Noel Keane, the infamous baby broker who boasted that he had made $300,000 in fees the year of the Baby M contract, has found another métier.

As our Eastern European friends are now reminding us, however, markets must be served. The New Jersey Supreme Court put a damper on Baby M–style contract motherhood —now known as "traditional surrogacy," as if it had come over with the Pilgrims—but it seems to have spurred science and commerce on to more ingenious devices. And so we have Baby Boy Johnson. Thanks to Baby M, we are a little sheepish, a little wiser. Ellen Goodman has called for the banning of gestational surrogacy for pay; like millions of other middle-aging moms, she wonders if being able to bear a child in one's fifties is really an unmitigated blessing. But we have not yet, as a society, begun to face the underlying ideas about class, race, children and, above all, women that the new maternities rely on.

Take class. By upholding the Johnson-Calvert contract, Judge Parslow opens the door to the sale of poor women's bodies to well-off couples. It is disingenuous to claim, as does Polly Craig of the Los Angeles Center for Surrogate Parenting, that $10,000 is not enough money to motivate a woman to sell her womb, and that gestational surrogates simply enjoy being pregnant, want to help others, or wish to atone for a past abortion. Why offer payment at all, if it serves no function? And why, if gestational surrogacy is such an occasion for pleasure, altruism and moral purification, don't prosperous women line up for it? The Calverts—she a nurse, he an insurance broker—presumably possess a wide female acquaintanceship in their own income bracket, none of whom felt friendship required of them that they turn over their bodies to the Calvertian zygote. Instead the couple approached Johnson, a sometime welfare recipient, single mother and low-paid worker at Crispina Calvert's hospital.

No, money is the motivator here. Ten thousand dollars may not seem like a lot to Craig and her clients, but it's a poor person's idea of major cash—as much as 25 percent of American women earn in a whole year of full-time employment. It's quite enough to becloud good judgment. "You wave $10,000 in front of someone's face," said Anna Johnson, "and they are going to jump for it." By "someone," Johnson meant women like herself, shuttling between welfare and dead-end jobs, single, already supporting a child, with a drawerful of bills and not much hope for the future.

In a particularly nasty wrinkle, gestational surrogacy invites the singling out of black women for exploitation. It's not just that blacks are disproportionately poor and desperate, more likely to be single mothers and more likely to lack the resources to sue. It's that their visible lack of genetic connection with the baby will argue powerfully against them in court. (Indeed, about the Baby Boy Johnson case hovers the suggestion that the Calverts chose Johnson for precisely this reason.) Judge Parslow's comparison of Johnson to a foster mother is interesting in view of the fact that foster mothers who grow attached to their charges and try to keep them are regarded with much popular sympathy and sometimes even succeed. But it is safe to say that few American judges are going to take seriously the claims of a black woman to a nonblack child. Black women have, after all, always raised white children without acquiring any rights to them. Now they can breed them, too.

There are those who worry about the social implications

of gestational surrogacy but who still think Judge Parslow made the right choice of homes for Baby Boy Johnson. Be that as it may, Anna Johnson wasn't suing for custody but for visitation. She wanted to be a small part of the child's life, for him to know her and for her to know him. Why would that be so terrible? As Dr. Michelle Harrison, who testified for Johnson, wrote in *The Wall Street Journal*, Judge Parslow wasn't being asked to divide the child between three parents; the Calverts had in fact so divided him when they chose to produce a baby with Johnson's help. Recent court decisions (not to mention social customs like open adoption, blended families and gay and lesbian co-parenting) have tended to respect a widening circle of adult relationships with children. Every state, for instance, gives grandparents access to grandchildren in the case of a divorce, regardless of the wishes of the custodial parent. Stepparents and lesbian co-parents are demanding their day in court. In 1986, California state courts upheld the right of a sperm donor to sue for parental rights when the artificial insemination did not involve a doctor (the old turkey-baster method). Why isn't *that* prospect too "crazy-making" for California? Or, for that matter, mandatory joint custody, an innovation that California pioneered? Given the increasing number of children living outside the classic nuclear-family arrangement, and the equanimity with which the courts divide them up among competing adults, it seems rather late in the day to get all stuffy about Anna Johnson.

The most important and distressing aspect of Judge Parslow's decision, however, is that it defines, or redefines, maternity in a way that is thoroughly degrading to women. By equating motherhood with fatherhood—that is, defining it solely as the contribution of genetic material—he has downgraded the mother's other contributions (carrying the fetus to term and giving birth) to services rather than integral components of biological parenthood. Under this legal definition, a normally pregnant woman is now baby-sitting for a fetus that happens to be her own. "In a debate over nature vs. nurture, the winner is nature" read the *New York Times* pull-quote. But why define "nature" as DNA rather than as the physiological events of pregnancy and birth? There's nothing "natural" about egg donation, which involves the hormonal priming of an infertile woman, the extraction of an egg by delicate technology, fertilization in a dish with masturbated sperm and implantation of the zygote in another. And to call pregnancy and childbirth "nurture" seems a feeble way to describe the sharing of the body and the risking of health, well-being and even life itself that is required to bring another life into existence. Like "parenting," another fashionable buzz-word, "nurture" is a bland social-sciency word that belittles a profound relationship and masks the role of women in gender-neutral language.

The picture of pregnancy as biological baby-sitting has many sources. It's as old as Aeschylus, who had Athena acquit Orestes of matricide in the *Eumenides* on the ground that mothers are merely "nurses" of men's seed, and as new as those ubiquitous photos of fetuses seeming to float in empty space. But its major proponents today are the antiabortionists. In order to maximize the claims of the fetus to personhood, they must obscure the unique status of the pregnant woman: She is not making a person, because the fertilized egg already *is* a person; she's only caring for it, or housing it, or even (as one imaginative federal judge recently wrote) holding it captive. Ironically, the movement that claims to celebrate motherhood is led by its own logic to devalue the physical, emotional and social experience of pregnancy. If unwanted pregnancy is just an "inconvenience," how serious an occasion can a *wanted* pregnancy be? If mass adoption is the answer to 1.6 million annual abortions, how strong can the ties be between mother and newborn? When ethicists fret that professional women may resort to gestational surrogacy to avoid "putting their careers on hold," they betray more than antiquated views about the capacities of pregnant women to get out of bed in the morning. They reveal their own assumption that pregnancy is a trivial, empty experience with nothing positive about it except the end product, the genetically connected baby. They then compound the insult by attributing this view to a demonized fantasy of working women—cold, materialistic, selfish, corrupted by "male values"—that is, those held by the ethicists themselves. Is there any evidence that working women—even M.B.A.s, even lawyers—see pregnancy this way? Who do the pundits think are mobbing infertility clinics and signing on for donated eggs? A couple needs two incomes just to pay the doctors.

Why is the primacy of genetics so attractive? At the moment, genetic determinism is having one of its periods of scientific fashion, fueling the fear that an adopted baby will never "really" be yours. At the same time, hardening class distinctions make the poor, who provide most adoptive babies, seem scary and doomed: What if junior took after his birth parents? It's not an accident that sperm donors and now egg donors are largely recruited among middle-class educated folk—they're not just white, they're successful and smart—and that the commercial aspects of the transaction ($50 for sperm, $1,500 for an egg) are disguised by calling it a "donation." You can buy a womb because wombs don't really matter, but if the all-important DNA must come from a third party, it should come as a gift between equals.

The main reason for our love affair with genes, though, is that men have them. We can't get all the way back to Aeschylus, with man as the seed sower and woman as flowerpot (although we acknowledge it in our language, when we call women "fertile" or "infertile," like farmland). Women, we now know, have seeds, too. But we can discount the aspects of procreation that women, and only women, perform. As the sociologist Barbara Katz Rothman has noted, Judge Parslow's decision follows the general pattern of our society, in which women's experiences are recognized to the extent that they are identical with men's, and devalued or ignored to the extent that they are different. Thus, Mary Beth Whitehead won back her parental rights because the New Jersey Supreme Court acknowledged her *genetic* contribution: Baby M was half hers. And the postmenopausally pregnant, egg-donated women achieve parental rights by being married to the babies' fathers, not through their own contributions.

Of the two practices—actually a single practice with two social constructions—gestational surrogacy is clearly the more repellent, but to see its real meaning it must be looked at with egg donation as its flip side. Taken together they bring pregnancy into line with other domestic tasks traditionally performed by women—housework, child care, sex. Performed within marriage, for no pay, these activities are slathered with sentimentality and declared beyond price, the cornerstone of female self-worth, family happiness and civilization itself. That is the world inhabited by prosperous married women now able to undergo pregnancy thanks to egg donation. That the egg is not their own is a detail; what counts is that they are able to have a profound and transforming life experience, to bond prenatally with their baby and to reproduce the genes of their husband. But look what happens when the checkbook and the marriage certificate are in the other hand: Now the egg is the central concern, pregnancy and childbirth merely a chore, prenatal bonding a myth. Like all domestic labor performed for pay—housecleaning, baby-sitting, prostitution —childbearing in the marketplace becomes disreputable work performed by suspect, marginal people. The priceless task turns out to have a price after all: about $1.50 an hour.

What should happen now? Some suggest that new methods

of parenthood require a new legal principle: pre-conception intent. Instead of socio-bio-ethical headaches—Who is the mother? Who is the father? What's best for the child? What's best for society?—we could have a simple rule of thumb: Let the seller beware. But at what cost to economic fairness, to principles of bodily integrity, to the nonmarketplace values that shape intimate life? Why not let the *buyer* beware? We cannot settle thorny questions by simply refusing to ask them.

A doctrine of pre-conception intent could, moreover, turn ordinary family law into fruit salad. Most pregnancies in the United States, after all, are not intended by either partner. They occur for dozens of reasons: birth-control failure, passion, ignorance, mixed messages, fear. The law wisely overlooks these sorry facts. Instead, it says Here is a child, here are the parents, next case. Do we really want to threaten a philosophy aimed, however clumsily, at protecting children from pauperism and abandonment? If pre-conception intent caught on with the general public, no single mother would be able to win child support; no single father could win parental rights. A woman's right to abortion could be conditioned on her pre-conception intent as evidenced, for example, by her use or neglect of birth control. In fact, in several states, laws have already been proposed that would restrict abortion to women who could prove contraceptive failure (a near impossibility, if you think about it, which is probably the point).

Perhaps the biggest problem with pre-conception intent, however, is that it ignores almost everything about the actual experience of becoming a parent of either sex. Planning to have a baby is not the same as being pregnant and giving birth, any more than putting on sexy underwear is like making love. The long months of pregnancy and the intense struggle of childbirth are part of forming a relationship with the child-to-be, part of the social and emotional task of parenthood. Not the only part, or even a necessary part—I am not suggesting that adoptive parents do not "really" become mothers and fathers. But is there a woman who feels exactly the same about the baby in the ninth month, or during delivery or immediately afterward, as she did when she threw away her diaphragm? When friends and relatives assure ambivalent parents-to-be not to worry, they'll feel differently about the baby when they feel it kick, or go through Lamaze together, or first hold their newborn in their arms, are they only talking through their hats? Whether or not there is a purely biological maternal instinct, more mothers, and more fathers, fall in love with their babies than ever thought they would. Indeed, if they did not, most babies would die of neglect in their cribs. How can we respect this emotional and psychological process—indeed, rely on it—and at the same time forbid it to the Mary Beth Whiteheads and the Anna Johnsons? I don't think we can.

Pre-conception intent would wreak havoc on everyone—men, women and children—and for what? To give couples like the Calverts a risk-free shot at a genetically connected baby. It makes more sense to assimilate surrogacy to already existing values and legal principles. In my view, doing so would make payment illegal and prebirth contracts unenforceable. We don't let people sell their organs or work at slave wages; we don't hold new mothers to predelivery adoption arrangements; we don't permit the sale of children; we don't enforce contracts that violate human dignity and human rights. We respect the role of emotion and change and second thoughts in private life: We let people jilt their fiancés, and we let them divorce their spouses. True, we uphold prenuptial agreements (a mistake, in my opinion), but they're about property. If someone signed a premarital agreement never to see his children again in the case of divorce, what judge would uphold it? Those children weren't even conceived when that contract was signed, the judge would point out—and furthermore they have rights that cannot be waived by others, such as the right to contact with both parents after divorce. The children of surrogates—even nongenetic surrogates like Anna Johnson—have the right to know the women through whose body and through whose efforts they came into the world. We don't need any more disposable relationships in the world of children. They have quite enough of those already.

In order to benefit a very small number of people—prosperous womb-infertile couples who shun adoption—paid surrogacy does a great deal of harm to the rest of us. It degrades women by devaluing pregnancy and childbirth; it degrades children by commercializing their creation; it degrades the poor by offering them a devil's bargain at bargain prices. It creates a whole new class of emotionally injured children rarely mentioned in the debate: the ones the surrogate has already given birth to, who see their mother give away a newborn, or fight not to.

It is hard for Americans to see why they shouldn't have what they want if they can pay for it. We would much rather talk about individual freedoms and property rights, rational self-interest and the supposed sanctity of contracts, than about the common good or human dignity, or the depths below which no person should be allowed to sink. But even we have to call it quits somewhere. As we decided 130 years ago, the buying and selling of people is a very good place to draw the line.

1990

Hot Flash

PMS. Postpartum psychosis. Breast implants. Breast cancer. Infertility. Bulimia/anorexia/dieting-for-life. There seems to be no end to the media's fascination with women's bodies. Thus, the last few weeks have seen a mysteriously synchronized spate of verbiage about, of all things, menopause: a multipart series in *The New York Times* and *Newsday*, a cover story in *Newsweek*, a piece in *USA Today*, Gail Sheehy's *The Silent Passage*, with Germaine Greer's *The Change* to follow in the fall. Invariably beginning with a tribute to upper-income baby-boom women—you know, educated medical consumers used to speaking out and getting what they want (Right. Like the ever-rising unnecessary-cesarean rate, I suppose), the articles move in swiftly for the kill: hot flashes, osteoporosis, irritability, heart disease, insomnia, migraines, declining libido, wrinkles and job loss. Job loss? *Newsweek*, the Backlash Bible (it recently published a cover story on sexual abuse of patients by therapists in which *all* the therapists pictured were female), actually unearthed a woman so discombobulated by menopause that she quit her "high-stress job" for something less taxing. So now you know why no women are running for President this year.

I'm not arguing that silence is golden. Clearly, it's better to have attention than patronizing neglect. It was fun to find *The New York Times*'s resident health nut Jane Brody recommending "a dildo" to menopausal women suffering from vaginal dryness (what's next: pornography? love affairs with actual human beings?). But with menopause, as with menstruation, childbirth and breast size, normal physiological conditions are being transformed into medical pathologies; symptoms that are incredibly rare are presented as typical; sociocultural explanations are slighted in favor of purely biological accounts; and finally, when women have been made sufficiently miserable and frightened, drugs, surgery, therapy and punitive diet-and-exercise regimes are offered as "cures"—in the case of menopause, lifelong estrogen supplements. Crone or guinea pig? "Women Must Decide," warns the *Times*. Procrastinate and die.

The underlying message in the news stories about women's health is always the same: Whether it's raging hormones or aging hormones, women are the victims of their bodies, except when, as with breast implants and eating disorders, they're the victims of neurotically distorted body images—images the media (the same outlets that bring you these distressing health bulletins) promote. Challenged, for example, to feature full-figured women to defuse the media-fed obsession with slimness, magazines now offer "more womanly" models: the same incredibly thin, tall post-teenagers, only with breast implants. I suppose the menopause obsession and the large market of "peri-menopausal" women will bring us a handful of "older" models: incredibly thin, tall, silver-haired, face-lifted beauties on estrogen.

It's hard not to read into the flurry of interest in menopause a kind of "so there" to fortysomething women, now, theoretically, in the prime of their work years. (No one, needless to say, is interested in the hot flashes of cleaning ladies and clerical workers, who presumably just mop their brows and keep on drudging.) You thought you could compete with men, you thought you could stay attractive, you thought you could thumb your nose at high-tech medicine. Well, ladies, time's up.

It would be nice if the focus on female physiology really was what its promoters claim: a feminist-inspired campaign for research dollars, public education and social understanding. But that's only one strand in a mix that includes misogynous canards, unrealistic beauty ideals and an uncritical—and dangerous—reliance on experimental medicine. The obsession with women's bodies is unfortunately not the same as rational concern for women's health. You would never guess from the news coverage that the major killer of women is not breast cancer but heart disease, with lung cancer moving up to first place on the cancer chart. Of course we need more and better breast-cancer treatments; of course it's a scandal that few insurance policies pay for mammograms and that, as a recent study showed, surgeons continue routinely to perform the discredited radical mastectomy. But something is out of whack when women who smoke are more terrified of breast cancer, about which they can do little, than lung cancer, which they can effectively prevent—and when one of the main reasons they continue to puff away is that they fear the modest weight gain often attendant on quitting. Something is out of whack when women prefer breasts of plastic and scar tissue to real ones of flesh and blood, as if experiencing sexual pleasure mattered less than presenting an image of sexiness. And something is out of whack when women who haven't eaten red meat in a decade sign on for lifetime hormone supplements about whose effects not nearly enough is known.

What's particularly infuriating about the medicalization of women's bodies is that it encourages a vision of men as the healthy, tranquil norm. If medicine and popular culture tend to see women in the old Aristotelian/Aquinian way—as deficient males, hampered at every turn by their messy, dangerous, cumbersome reproductive systems—they tend equally to gloss over the fact that men have reproductive systems, too. Look how long it took for male infertility, and the male contribution to birth defects, to be acknowledged as problems. And when was the last time you read a front-page article about prostate cancer—much less one illustrated with a photograph of a naked man?

Culturally, only women are defined, and define themselves, by their sexuality, as packaged for them by a sexist society. No one would dream of altering problematic male behaviors—hyperaggression and violence, for example—by medicating the entire sex, as is now being proposed, on much less provocation, for my generation of women. Men wouldn't put up with it, and I don't blame them. Indeed, when it comes to their bodies, the famously fragile male ego seems amazingly robust. While women by the million-plus have had breast implants, exactly *one* man has had experimental surgery to lengthen his penis; he made the talk shows, which is how I know. And remember Rogaine? It turns out that this "cure" for baldness—which supposedly worries and embarrasses men as a visible sign of aging—didn't go over too well with men: It required too much effort, cost too much and didn't work very well. The manufacturers are now shifting their target market to women with "thin hair."

They'll probably make a fortune.

1992

Who's Afraid of Hillary Clinton?

T ed Koppel is not exactly known for in-depth coverage of
the issues, but in March he came across a story so big,
so urgent, so far-reaching in its implications for democracy
that he needed two entire sessions of "Nightline" to reveal its
full dimensions to the American people. Atrocities in Angola?
One in ten Americans on food stamps? Why Johnny still can't
read? Don't be silly. The topic was Hillary Clinton. Does she
have too much power, or what?

Having noted for the record that the First Lady enjoys
healthy approval ratings in the polls, and that two-thirds of the
population sees nothing amiss with her chairing the Administration's task force on health care, and having further noted
that most of her critics are white men and Republicans, Koppel
devoted the bulk of both shows to conducting a chorus of complaints from members of those overlapping disgruntled minorities. Sound bites from Mickey Kaus, Rush Limbaugh, Robert
Novak, Thomas Mann (the Brookings Institution heavy, not

the German novelist) and others built up the now familiar media cartoon: Hillary Rodham Clinton as the overbearing wife with a finger in every slice of government pie, a workaholic ideologue accountable to no one but her pussywhipped husband, an "unelected consort" in a "quasi-monarchical relationship," who promotes the hiring of women, like Donna Shalala, from her circle of hyperliberal friends. Kaus noted that her influence is felt even in an "obscure federal agency" like the Resolution Trust Corporation, where people are "scared" of her: "Imagine how strong her influence is on the more obvious agencies!"

"This is not some kind of a woman behind the scenes who's pulling the strings," said Michael Deaver, clearly nostalgic for the astrological management style of his erstwhile employer Nancy Reagan. "This woman's out front pulling the strings."

While Ms. Clinton's attackers were prominent figures, named and given plenty of air time, her defenders were mostly lightweights (the managing editor of *People*) or anonymous (a Japanese woman, who said through an interpreter, "I hope I can be like her when I reach her age"). Only two women were quoted more than once: Washington style-watcher Sally Quinn, herself a power wife of note, and feminist columnist Ellen Goodman, both of whom spoke in generalities about marriage. The whole debate, indeed, was structured as a kind of contest between *Redbook* and *The Wilson Quarterly*, girl talk and fluff versus the threat to the Republic: Should America go down the tubes so that the tea-serving secretaries of Tokyo can have a positive role model? And just in case the viewer might be inclined to say, Sure, why not?, Koppel was quick to sound an ominous note: "When we come back, the question, What if the President thinks the First Lady is doing a bad job?" Short of putting her into an insulin coma, the answer was, He's stuck. After all, they're married.

Poor H.R.C. Perhaps she thought her husband's victory

would put paid to the nitpicking and bitchiness and ponderous rumblings about the First Lady's "role" which swirled around her during the campaign. All summer long the lifestyle industry churned out articles with titles like "Are We Ready for a First Lady as First Partner?" (All right, I admit it, I wrote that one, for *Glamour*.) You'd think the election would have answered that question. But no, the media mill grinds on. There was the Inaugural hat disaster, the dropping of the strategically assumed adoring gaze at Bill, the readoption of Rodham as a middle name. What with all the headscratching and thumbsucking that these provoked, you would never know that in the United States today hundreds of thousands of married women do not assume their husband's surname, that 12 percent of the armed forces and 42 percent of law students are women, that 59 percent of married couples have two wage earners and that in 21 percent of those couples the wife earns more than her husband.

Now that she's actually ensconced in the White House, the First Lady has become a quasi-pornographic obsession, exemplified by *Spy*, which put her on its cover in leather with a whip and a manic grin: the First Dominatrix. There are dirty jokes, sexist jokes and sexual rumors galore: H.R.C. is a lesbian, currently conducting an affair with a well-known actress; she's got Bill in some incredible sexual stranglehold. Any doubts that the Clinton Administration is the most open in living memory should be assuaged by the fact that *everyone* knows, or thinks he knows, what goes on in the Lincoln Bedroom: the lamp- (or Bible-, or urn-) throwing incident (*Newsweek* actually printed this one), the blackmailing-Bill-with-girlfriends-yet-unknown theory, the no-sex-for-the-past-five-years rumor. It was another mom from my daughter's kindergarten who filled me in on the absence of action in the presidential bed. Talk about six degrees of separation. From the White House to the Lab School, it's more like three.

Now, at this point I must say that I am no fan of Hillary Rodham Clinton's politics. I'm a single-payer health care system supporter, myself. I don't like some of the compromises she's made on social issues, either: What kind of children's rights advocate, after all, supports parental notification on abortion? If you pulled out enough of my fingernails, I'd probably admit that I think a wife who takes her husband's name is a wimp, especially if, like Hillary, she does so to make her guy look macho. I'd even admit that there's something sad about the fact that the most powerful woman to emerge from the much-ballyhooed Year of the Woman is a wife. This is the "false feminist" issue raised by Mickey Kaus, who, like most people who raise this objection to Hillary's activism, is no great fan of real feminists. Hillary, by this line, is just piggybacking off Bill instead of relying on her own efforts.

There's no denying that wifehood sometimes confers unfair advantages. But so too does being a husband. Indeed, one of Bill Clinton's likable qualities is that he publicly acknowledges the part his wife's brains and energy have played in his own career. We do not live in a society composed of autonomous monads. In fact, we live in a society that has in very large measure decided to distribute its goods through the family system, whether it's health insurance, Social Security, money or party invitations. (Well, rumor has it that when Isaac Bashevis Singer won the Nobel Prize in Literature, he flew first-class to Stockholm and made his wife fly coach, but you see my point.) But when a man benefits through his wife, we tend to close our eyes; when a woman benefits through her husband, we assume she's otherwise "unqualified." Marty Peretz and Frances Lear both own magazines bought with their spouse's money. But while Lear was ridiculed in the press when she started *Lear's* with her divorce settlement millions—she was an egomaniac, a greedy alimony queen who knew nothing about magazines, etc., etc.—nobody questioned the validity of Peretz's buying *The New Republic* with his wife's inherited wealth or mocked his ambitions as inappropriate for an academic. As it turns out, both magazines are quite successful, but only Lear had to overcome a presumption that her position was illegitimate and that she herself was a fool, perhaps because at some level we still believe that marital money is really the husband's, no matter whose name is on the stocks and bonds, and whatever the community property statutes say.

Hillary's detractors make a great fuss over the fact that she was not elected. That is true. But no one who serves in a presidential administration is elected except the Vice President. At least with the Clinton Administration the electorate was apprised in advance that Hillary would play some sort of political role, so if people couldn't live with that, they could choose to vote for George and Barbara. With the Reagans, on the other hand, the fact that the First Lady would wield considerable power was actively concealed from the people. Why is it so dreadful that Hillary helps Bill make his appointments but not that, say, J.F.K.'s father—the ex-bootlegger and Nazi sympathizer—helped him compose his Cabinet? (Now, if it had been Rose Kennedy providing the advice, we'd *never* have heard the end of it.) True, J.F.K. took a lot of flak for naming his brother Attorney General, and Congress promptly passed an antinepotism law, which Hillary's own position risks flouting. The two cases aren't really comparable—head of the health care task force is hardly a Cabinet-level position—but taken together they suggest that we rethink the whole subject. Maybe it *isn't* worse to give an Administration position to a presidential relative than to a presidential crony or big-money contributor.

Maybe the President should be permitted, as constitutional precedent suggests, to take appropriate counsel from those he sees fit to consult. As for the objection that Bill can't fire

Hillary, well, sure he can—although it would doubtless be presented to the public as something else. Certainly nobody thinks that Bill will feel compelled to implement the findings of Hillary's task force if, by some bizarre chance, it comes up with a plan he disdains.

It's funny how those who recoil at Hillary's position in the Administration return to the old comic view of marriage, in which any husband more congenial than Genghis Khan is assumed to be putty in the hands of his wife, and any wife less demure than Pat Nixon is assumed to be a shrew. A Republican operative said the Bush campaign planned to show that Bill Clinton is "out of control" and "can't control his zipper, can't control his wife and can't control his waistline." In women, power is always seen as connected, in some way or other, with sex, even if no one can figure out exactly what the connection is. That's why people can half-believe all the rumors about Hillary, mutually exclusive though they be: let's see, a lamp-throwing lesbian who enslaves her husband by refusing to exercise on his person the amazing sexual power she has over him despite his appetite for other women, with which she is blackmailing him. All this in order to run a policy-wonkery show trial, whose verdict—managed competition, yes!—was in at the start. You'd think the paragon who could pull off this complicated gambit would hold out for Secretary of State.

The sexist attack on Hillary Clinton is partly a lazy way to attack her husband, of course. I doubt Rush Limbaugh would be playing "Hail to the Chief" at the mention of the First Lady's name if she were heading up a presidential task force to abolish affirmative action and build a wall on the Mexican border. Similarly, would Mickey Kaus object to Hillary's interest in the Resolution Trust Corporation if she did not support the "paleoliberal" notion that the property belonging to failed S&Ls should be sold off at modest prices to ordinary people?

From Marie Antoinette to Joy Silverman (whom you may remember as the obsessive-love object of jilted New York State Appeals Court Judge Sol Wachtler, and whom no less a free spirit than Bill Kunstler called a "Republican whore"), misogyny and sexual slurs provide a handy shorthand with which to express one's hostility to a woman's—or her husband's—politics. But it is also true that the politics and the image of the Clinton Administration are closely bound up with issues of gender: the social shift to more egalitarian marriages; the growing political power of women, who voted for Bill Clinton by an eight-point margin, two and a half times that of male voters; the mainstreaming of a popular you-can-do-it feminism; and a wellspring of support, disproportionately female, for renewed government activism in the domestic sphere—what conservatives, interestingly, like to deride as "the nanny state." Attacking H.R.C. is a way of attacking these broad social and political transformations without actually making a case against them. Because, as we saw from the reaction to Marilyn Quayle's speech about women's "essential nature" and Pat Buchanan's call for a cultural war, that case has already been lost.

The fact is, as even Koppel admitted, H.R.C. is an immensely popular figure: The January *People* with her picture on the cover outsold all issues since last June's "DIANA: Dramatic Excerpts From the Book That Rocked Britain." Even *Ladies' Home Journal* touts her for ushering in the "Age of the Smart Woman." So who has a Hillary problem? The media.

"It makes me sick the way journalists go after Hillary," one male *Newsday* editor told me. "And what's weird about it is they're baby boomers—sophisticated guys who've lived with feminism for twenty years." There's a Freudian explanation for the media's zeal: The Clintons are the first First Family from the boomers' own generation, thus freeing fortysomethings to express their envy and hostility toward those in power: Who do the Clintons think they are? And there's a political explanation: The Reagan/Bush years moved the press in an increasingly rightward direction—the metamorphosis of Joe Klein from sympathetic Woody Guthrie biographer to "family values" harrumpher is the paradigmatic case—which, like the path of an ocean liner, it will take ages to reverse.

And then there's my own pet theory: The anti-Hillary media types, for the most part men, are protecting their turf. (The female snipers are just jealous.) Despite its reputation as *la carrière ouverte aux talents*, journalism is actually one of the last bastions of old-fashioned irrational male privilege. This year, as in past years, the research project Women, Men & Media found that newspapers and television news programs overwhelmingly featured male reporters, male commentators, male experts and interviewees. The table of contents of virtually every magazine of news and opinion tells the same story. While women have managed to eke out a small preserve in feminist-oriented Op-Ed columns—Anna Quindlen, Ellen Goodman, Judy Mann and many others—the Big Beats belong to the big boys. There is no female counterpart to the phony-proletarian big-city-ethnic columnists like Jimmy Breslin, Mike Royko, Mike McAlary and Mike Barnicle (although Amy Pagnozzi is a contender); no female opinionmeister with the week-in, week-out visibility and ideological clout of Joe Klein or Mickey Kaus or Michael Kinsley or John Leo or John Taylor. Journalism, of course, is hardly the only male-dominated profession. But it's the only one that has no official credentialing system by which women can either be kept out (major league sports, the priesthood) or, after successfully completing a set of formal requirements, insist on admittance (law, medicine, the Protestant clergy). Journalism degrees don't count for much; everyone knows all you need is a talent for quick opinions and clever phrases and an ability to meet a deadline, gifts even their most ardent detractors concede women have in spades! There's no good reason that women shouldn't assume the same prominent position in journalism that they now have in the world of books—think of all the important new women novelists, poets, essayists, editors. The more women excel in other fields the harder it is to explain their marginality in the press as anything but what it is—sex discrimination.

Could it be that the anti-Hillary pundits and talking heads are motivated by status anxiety and fear for their jobs? She may not have been elected, but what if nobody cares? She's a lot more qualified than most of the people giving her advice in the media. She just *might* usher in that Age of the Smart Woman. And where will the Joe Kleins and Mickey Kauses be then?

Ted Koppel worries about what Bill will do if Hillary does a bad job. He ought to be worrying about what he himself will do if she does a good job, and Cokie Roberts decides she'd like a shot at his.

1993

The Romantic Climacteric

It seems only yesterday that Germaine Greer was exhorting young women to throw away their inhibitions, their engagement rings and their underpants. With the publication of *The Female Eunuch*, in 1970, Greer burst into international celebrity—an inescapable media presence, brash, brilliant and beautiful, as exotically plumed as some wild Australian bird and equally given to preening. Her love affairs were legendary, her admonitions—Flaunt your tampons! Taste your menstrual blood! Stop expecting men to take care of you! Live!—a heady mixture of rebellion and flirtatiousness. While the press, then as now, delighted to portray the women's movement as motivated by hatred of men and led by frumps and neurotics, it made an exception for Greer. She was, as *Life* put it, the "saucy feminist even men like," and the one who never let men forget how much she liked them.

Well, that was then; this is now. Having publicly mourned

her inability to get pregnant in her forties—and having produced *Sex and Destiny*, an anticontraception polemic and paean to Third World motherhood—Greer has passed through menopause and emerged, in her early fifties, on the other side. It was hardly to be expected that she would experience the transition calmly: Rage and passion have always been her strong suits. (Indeed, since *Sex and Destiny* they have sometimes seemed to be her only suits.) Still, among the millions of female baby boomers now moving toward middle age there must be many whose hearts leaped up when they beheld the publisher's announcement of *The Change: Women, Aging and the Menopause*. Who better than Greer to deploy a fiery contrarian sword against society's contempt for older women, drug-company hormone pushing and the hand-wringing to be found in Gail Sheehy's best-selling *The Silent Passage*, in which woman after woman mops her hot-flashing brow and wails "Why can't I be me anymore?"

Greer does brandish a fiery contrarian sword in *The Change*. But something has gone terribly wrong. Perhaps she dashed the book off too quickly: repeated sentences, haphazard organization, the grab-bag inclusion of irrelevant material (a five-page bone-dry synopsis of Iris Murdoch's novel *Bruno's Dream*, for instance), all suggest a rush to publish. Or perhaps she was overwhelmed by the scope of her task—disputing just about everything that has been thought, said, written and done regarding women and age for the last two hundred years— and lost the thread of her arguments in the general contentiousness. That would explain why she could spend pages excoriating doctors for handing out estrogen like candy and then, noting that the hormone does seem to make women feel better, reverse gears and "question the morality" of withholding it. In any case, *The Change* is a maddening and frustrating book, in which passages of brilliance, wit and lyricism alternate with murky and carelessly reported science, crackpot health advice and a portrait of modern female aging that goes well beyond the evidence in its gloom and despair. And that, given the real difficulties that women face as they get older, is saying a lot.

The Change begins promisingly, with a rousing indictment of modern attitudes toward older women. Greer notes with some bitterness that our supposedly youth-crazed culture is really a girl-crazed culture: men acquire social power along with wrinkles and gray hair, and often a young bride or mistress, too, while their female contemporaries are often consigned to the sexual scrap heap, if not, indeed, the poorhouse. She quotes a friend on the May-November couples around them in a restaurant. " 'It's bloody unfair. Those men can have their pick of women of any age. They can go on for years, and here we are, finished. They wouldn't even look at us.' The unkind sunlight showed every sag, every pucker, every bluish shadow, every mole, every freckle in our fifty-year-old faces. When we beckoned to the waiter he seemed not to see us."

Greer has a word for what she thinks that waiter feels: "anophobia," the irrational fear and hatred of old women. In many preindustrial societies, she argues in a somewhat hedged reprise of *Sex and Destiny*, older women are vigorous and respected members of extended families, and, while ultimately subject to men, wield a good deal of informal social power. It is only in the modern West, where women are valued primarily as sex objects, families are small and isolated, and "hostility to the mother . . . is an index of mental health," that the aging woman is an outcast—expected to be unobtrusive, compliant, and grateful for any crumbs of attention that fall her way. Eventually, when he has nothing better to do, that waiter will amble over to her table.

Surrounded as women are by the negative stereotypes of popular culture—harridan mothers-in-law, strident shoppers, comical grandmas—and facing, moreover, the actual fact of their declining value in the sexual marketplace, it's hardly surprising that many regard the prospect of aging with anxiety, or that a vast beauty-exercise-surgery-quackery industry has arisen to exploit their fears while seeming to soothe them. Today, women are told that with enough effort, time and, of course, money the years need hold no terrors: Celebrities like Jane Fonda, Cher and Joan Collins are touted—and tout themselves—as proof. But, as Greer shrewdly points out, the cult of these bionic sexpots only reinforces the prejudice against the aging female. To urge women to ape youth with an "imitation body" is to declare unacceptable the body they really have.

No wonder the male-dominated medical establishment regards menopause as a trauma and a tragedy. It marks the end of a woman's usefulness to men, and since in Greer's view society permits her no other purpose, doctors are quick to offer, and some women to accept, alarming remedies. (Greer has a scary chapter on the history of useless, painful and sometimes even fatal treatments for menopause: electric shocks to the womb, X rays, animal-gland extracts, hysterectomy, hormone cocktails.) A woman who finds menopause rough going is invariably blamed for her symptoms: She had no children or was "overinvested" in maternity; dulled herself with domesticity or masculinized herself in the workplace; staked all on romance or failed to make hay while the sun shone. Declining sexual interest in middle-aged marriages is perceived as the woman's problem: If her husband withdraws, it's because she is sagging and nagging; if she does, it's her hormones. Why not, Greer pointedly inquires, ask if the man is a sensitive lover, an affectionate and respectful partner?

Maybe *he* has let himself go: "Many a man who was attractive and amusing at twenty is a pompous old bore at fifty." If intercourse has become painful (at menopause the vaginal walls become thinner and drier), why dose the woman with potentially dangerous hormones so that she can have more bad sex, instead of proposing more imaginative ways of lovemaking—or just letting her call it quits?

That, in fact, is Greer's suggestion to women: Give up. It's degrading to turn yourself into a geisha for a man who thinks he's doing you a favor by sticking around. Anyway, it won't work. No one mistakes a chemical peel for the rose-petal skin of youth. To the plaintive question "Is one never in this life to be allowed to let oneself go?" Greer offers a bold answer: Yes! Right now! Today!

Greer wants women to welcome menopause—she prefers the old-fashioned term "climacteric"—as a sweeping natural transition. Yes, it is physically turbulent: Like Sheehy, Greer dismisses women who pass through it easily—the vast majority, actually, although you'd never know it from either writer—as anomalous, if not liars. And, yes, it is sad: a time to take stock, to mourn old losses and to come to terms with death. But it also holds out the promise of freedom and tranquillity: "Autumn can be golden, milder and warmer than summer, and it is the most productive season of the year." Rejected by men, and thus freed from "the white slavery of attraction duty," the female eunuch can become, at last, "the female woman": a sibyl, a witch, a crone.

Greer's portrait of cronehood is so charming, so spirited, so seductively rendered—especially when it's contrasted with the situation of the wistful wives, desperate party girls and breast-implanted exercise addicts which for her constitutes the only alternative—that the reader may find herself barely able to wait. Why *not* take up nature study, herbal medicine, travel, contemplation? Make women friends—and a fuss if you're ignored by the waiter! One notes a certain class bias here, an assumption of leisure and posh tastes: no bowling, or volunteering at the local hospital—or, apparently, earning a living, either. There's an anti-intellectual bias, too: The graying Eternal Feminine is not to sign up for classes at the New School. Still, who wouldn't like to sink into the Bath for Melancholy she cites from an Old English receipt book ("Take mallowes pellitory of the wall, of each three handfulls; Camomell flowers, Mellelot flowers, of each one handfull; hollyhocks two handfulls")? Or stroll beside the sea with a girlhood chum, like the Sicilian matrons who, before the days of tourism, had the island beaches to themselves? Or start a huge garden, like Lady Mary Wortley Montagu—or Greer, a famous gardener herself? Greer calls us to middle age as to a grand spiritual adventure, and one with distinguished literary antecedents, too. This must be the only book ever written on women's health that illustrates its advice with seventeenth-century poetry and the letters of Mme. de Sévigné.

But there's a catch—several catches, actually. The would-be crone must become her own doctor—a dangerous prospect if she uses Greer's incomprehensible chapters on herbal and homeopathic medicine as a guide. (Henbane, for example, is a sedative on one page and a poison on another.) She must follow a diet that seems punitive in its frugality. (Giving up smoking and hard drinking makes sense, but red meat, cheese, coffee, tea, wine, beer and chocolate?)

And—but perhaps you suspected this was coming—barring a miracle, she must give up sex. Now, this is indeed strange, because Greer herself presents a whole gallery of celebrated women who, without benefit of plastic surgery, found romance in midlife and beyond. It is almost as though she began *The Change* with the idea of championing mature female sexuality—a casual reader might even think she has done so—and suddenly reversed herself in mid-book. One way or another, she dismantles her shining examples: In Colette's last years, her much younger husband never saw her "devastated body" or her face without its "powdered mask"; George Eliot's husband jumped out of the window on their honeymoon; Elizabeth Barrett Browning grew disenchanted with her Robert; Simone de Beauvoir's midlife affair with Claude Lanzmann "fizzled out" after ten years. "Fizzled out" seems an odd term in this context—a decade is not exactly a summer romance—but it shows how determined Greer is to take a negative view of middle-aged sexuality. For men and women alike, it is unaesthetic and faintly grotesque, but for women it is also potentially tragic, because it exposes them to humiliation and exploitation at the hands of layabouts, philanderers, bisexual flirts and neurasthenics. Who else, the clear implication runs, would even pretend to be interested? The women whose libido vanishes with menopause are, for Greer, "the lucky ones."

Could it be that Greer is a bit of an anophobe herself? Certainly she seems in a hurry to hustle women out of the bedroom and into the herb garden: By the end of *The Change*, she is lauding peasant cultures in which women don the black dress of matronly celibacy at thirty-five. One waits in vain for her to make the obvious rejoinder to our culture's hard view of older women's sexuality, to challenge the equation of female attractiveness with youth. Why, after all, should a lined face and gray hair not connote in women, as they do in men, experience, strength, staying power, character, sexual self-knowledge? Must older women give up being sexual subjects because Hollywood casting directors do not regard them as sexual objects? Greer cannot challenge the dominant masculine view because, in her heart, she shares it. The best she can do is caricature middle-aged men as "fat, beefy, beery, smelly, tobacco-stained" satyrs and recommend that older women who absolutely can't do without sex take boys (or women) as lovers.

How accurate is the picture of contemporary female middle-age presented in *The Change*? Although Greer's books are packed with data, she has never let inconvenient facts stand in the way of her enthusiasms. In *The Female Eunuch*, sex had to hold no dangers, and so she pooh-poohed domestic violence as mostly idle threats that the occasional foolhardy woman drove her man to carry out. (The basis of this extraordinary assertion? Greer's affairs with two young roughnecks, who, despite their criminal records, behaved like perfect gentlemen.) *Sex and Destiny*'s romantic portrait of Third World womanly life dismissed clitoridectomy—inflicted on millions of African, Asian and Middle Eastern girls each year—in a single sentence. *The Change*, too, ignores reality when it contradicts theory—only this time it's the good news, not the bad, that gets left out.

So, for the record, numerous studies demonstrate that most menopausal women do not, as Greer thinks, regard the cessation of ovulation with anguish or dread, do not undergo bouts of irrationality and rage, and do not lose their libido, their partner, or both. Middle-aged women are actually a fairly cheerful group—perhaps because few of them are living the contracted, empty-nest, husband-focused domestic life that Greer imagines is still the contemporary norm. Nor is middle-aged and elderly married sex typically the quasi rape Greer imagines, in which a dirty old man subjects his estrogen-drugged wife to beastly practices while he fantasizes about young girls. According to one recent study, couples who make love after sixty are the happiest in America, and the more they make love—and not just in the missionary position, either—the happier they are.

It is curious that Greer, who began her career as a sexual

swashbuckler, should end up preaching celibacy. There are doubtless many who will see this intellectual trajectory as a powerful rebuke to feminist hopes of equality. If biology is the culprit—if men are programmed to desire only youth and fertility, and if estrogen, as Greer claims in a particularly paranoid passage, is the "biddability" hormone that keeps women under the male thumb during the childbearing years —then sexism really is destiny, from which menopause is the sole hope of escape. But a feminism that can envision freedom and self-determination only at the margins of the female life cycle—before twelve and after fifty—has surely taken a wrong turn somewhere.

Yet Greer has never really been a feminist, although the media labeled her one. She has no interest in political action or collective solutions to individual problems, no skepticism toward essentialist accounts of gender difference, and no hope that men can change their personal priorities or that women can obtain an equal share of economic or political power—the "spiritual" power of cronehood is the best women can manage. What she is is a romantic egotist—a dramatizer of her own exemplary life—and a critic of modernity. In the former capacity, she resembles no one so much as her old antagonist Norman Mailer; in the latter, the Mexican priest and sociologist Ivan Illich, whose attacks on Western medicine and Western feminism her own work closely parallels. She has never been able to hold all the aspects of women's lives—sex, maternity, work, love, domesticity, passion, reason—in her mind at the same time. She has always seen feminism through the lens of her most recent life crisis, and called on all women to jettison whatever hopes and behaviors have just proved problematical for her. When she was a sexual freebooter, monogamy and children were traps. When she wanted a child, contraception and sexual egalitarianism were suddenly rationalist plots against nature's plan for true female happiness.

Now, as she has repeatedly announced, she's through with the whole business—sex, romance, men—and so we must all hang up our spurs and join her in a nice cup of henbane. *The Change* is an original and provocative book. But the only woman who is fully reflected in its pages is the one who wrote it.

1992

Our Right-to-Lifer:
The Mind of an Antiabortionist

When I first heard that an antiabortion demonstrator
had stationed himself outside the building in which
The Nation has its offices—a building that houses, among other
businesses and concerns, a gynecological clinic that performs
abortions—I had an immediate image of what he would look
like. He would be pale and rawboned and strained, a hungry
fanatic in a cheap suit, like a street-corner preacher in a Flan-
nery O'Connor story. What sort of person, after all, takes it
upon himself to stand alone on the street, day after day, and
thrust gory pictures of bloody fetuses at strangers while shouting "You're killing an innocent baby"?

I was wrong about the details. The demonstrator—perhaps
"harasser" is a better word given what he does—wears his
hair in a long ponytail and, in his blue jeans and parka, looks
like a pudgy hippie. He has beautiful green eyes, smiles easily
and seems less strained than phlegmatic and unfocused. His
name, he told me, is Ramon; he's thirty-two, unmarried, child-

less; he drives a bakery truck at night and lives alone in Jamaica, Queens. I was right about the main thing, though: He is a religious fanatic.

I had two longish talks with Ramon, punctuated by his calling out "Abortion is murder!" every few minutes as another woman brushed by him on her way into the building. They were not very satisfying conversations. For one thing, Ramon is evasive about facts: his last name, for instance, and his nationality. When I asked him if he had voted in the last election, he told me he was not a U.S. citizen but would not tell me what country he was from, except that it was in Latin America, and he pulled out a plastic rosary. "The Blessed Mother sent me here." What did his parents think of what he was doing? "The Blessed Mother and Jesus Christ are my parents."

For another thing, Ramon is not very intelligent. If you ask him a pointed question, he just goes silent. "The Bible says you're a human being," he told me, "even when you're just an egg, just a piece of mucus." When I asked him where the Bible said that (in fact, the Bible doesn't mention abortion at all, let alone eggs and mucus), he just looked sheepish. Should Jews and Protestants, whose religions permit abortion, have to abide by Catholic doctrine, which forbids it? Ramon stared off into space for what seemed like a very long time. "You know I can't answer all these deep questions," he said finally, sighing.

Ramon goes to Mass in a regular parish church, but his spiritual center is the old Vatican Pavilion at the 1964 World's Fair grounds in Flushing. There, marathon vigils are held by the followers of Veronica Lueken, the seer of Bayside, Queens—known in the movement as the Lourdes of America. Lueken, a middle-aged housewife and mother of five, claims that since 1970 she has been receiving visits from the Virgin Mary, who inveighs against Communism, homosexuality, abortion, rock music, drugs, feminism and the liturgical reforms of Vatican II, and who predicts the imminent end of the world in nuclear war and a "chastising comet." Although the church does not recognize the validity of Lueken's visions, she seems to have a following. (I've heard she's particularly popular in Quebec.) Her supporters were prominent in the picketing of Jean-Luc Godard's *Hail Mary* when it played in New York City in 1984.

Ramon gave me some of Lueken's literature, which is full of testimonials about wondrous cures connected with the Vatican Pavilion and is illustrated with "miraculous photos" showing squiggles of light around a statue of Mary. ("Thousands have been taken during the Vigils by various Polaroid cameras which produce 'tamper-proof' photos. Rosaries have turned from their natural metallic color to gold during the Vigils, the substance of gold having been verified by jewelers.") He thinks Veronica Lueken is a saint and is philosophical about the church's failure to acknowledge her visions. "The hierarchy has always been kind of slow," he confided with a rueful shrug. "You know what they're like."

Ramon's devotion to Lueken may put him on the theological fringe, at least for now, but his beliefs about abortion fall squarely within church doctrine—his opposition to abortion or contraception to preserve a woman's health or life, for instance. When I told him about a married acquaintance of mine who, at thirty-six, had a near-fatal heart attack and who now must be sterilized because pregnancy would kill her, Ramon suggested that she and her husband just give up sex. Well, I said, she could be raped; what about that? Silence. But what could he say? Wasn't one of the charges against Seattle Archbishop Raymond Hunthausen that he permitted therapeutic sterilization (of non-Catholics, mind you) in Catholic hospitals?

Again like the hierarchy, Ramon opposes birth control,

which he considers a form of murder. "Sex is for two married people who are comfortable with each other and are ready for a child." Then isn't so-called natural family planning a kind of murder, too, even though the church swears by it, since the whole idea there is to have sex only at (theoretically) unfertile times? Silence. I doubt that New York's Archbishop, John Cardinal O'Connor, could do much better.

You would think that Ramon would be bursting with intense emotion—anger, hatred, compassion, despair—toward the women he accosts. From his point of view, after all, they are figures in a high moral drama—souls in peril and potential murderers, Faust and Lady Macbeth in one. Yet he seems quite incurious about them and their situation. I had heard that he singled out young black and Hispanic women for his attentions, and although he dismissed that suggestion as ridiculous ("Hey, I'm Spanish myself!"), skin color and youth did seem to be his chief criteria while I was there. Beyond this crude attempt at identification, he did not seem to have considered at all what sort of people he was dealing with. When I asked him if he had ever dissuaded anyone from going through with her abortion, he immediately said, "Oh, yes, sure," as though it happened all the time. But when I asked for details, he modified his claim to "I think some of them read the pamphlets and think about it while they're waiting and change their minds."

"So you don't think women give this decision a lot of thought beforehand?"

"No. They don't think it through."

Only one woman took Ramon's literature while I was talking with him. Most seemed to ignore his shouts, hurrying quickly into the lobby with their faces carefully blank. But, then, most of the women entering the building are not going to the clinic, and many of the women who are going to the clinic aren't going for abortions. Given Ramon's presence, it is probably just as well that they aren't. I wonder how I would respond to his pamphlets, with their weird mélange of bloody photographs, bathetic morality tales and fraudulent statistics, were they to be thrust into my hand at such a moment. According to a booklet titled "Who Killed Junior?" for instance, "abortions are more than twice as dangerous as childbirth (U.S. Bureau of Vital Stastics [*sic*])"; "one in three teenage abortions have complications which might prevent the girl from having children again (study at Toronto, Canada, 1970)"; and "more than one-third of mothers of aborted babies have mental problems later (total of several Japanese studies)." I know that none of those statements are true. What if I believed them?

And what about the cards Ramon passes out for organizations such as AAA Pregnancy Problem Services, Options and Manhattan Pregnancy Services? More subtly deceptive than the pamphlets, they use the guarded language of television advertisements to appear to promise all manner of aid and comfort to desperate pregnant women: "Help arrange financial assistance"; "Show how you can continue school or job." Although listed in the Yellow Pages under "Clinics," these places have no doctors on staff and offer no medical services beyond administering home-kit pregnancy tests. According to the National Organization for Women, they are antiabortion advocacy centers masquerading as abortion clinics in order to attract naïve young women to their premises, where they can be frightened away from abortions, or even be given false information to cause them to postpone abortion until it's too late.

Out of curiosity, I called Birthline Hotline ("trained volunteers lend a sympathetic ear") when I got home. "How long do you have to wait after you miss your period before you can have a pregnancy test?" I asked in what I hoped was an anxious quaver. "Oh, a good long while, I'd say," replied a hearty female voice, "a good few weeks." I called again with the same question a couple of days later. This time I got a woman who said she was a nurse. Two weeks, she told me, and, furthermore, studies have shown that my boyfriend, or whoever he was, would leave me if I had an abortion, which is a very dangerous operation both physically and mentally, a fact obscured by state regulations which count a broken leg during pregnancy as a childbirth-related complication but don't count hepatitis from a blood transfusion during an abortion as an abortion-related complication, because abortion is a big for-profit industry. So much for trained volunteers.

My discussions with Ramon left me with mixed feelings. There was a certain elation, I admit, at having all my beliefs about the antiabortion movement so neatly confirmed in a single person: that it is essentially a reactionary religious crusade, opposed to nonprocreative sex and contraception, indifferent to the health and individual circumstances of women, bone-ignorant about their bodies and possessing only the haziest understanding of the difference between a papal encyclical and the laws of the state of New York. The comment of Ramon's I found myself returning to was "Sex is for two married people who feel comfortable with each other and who are ready for a child," with its assumption that discomfort and anxiety are the usual accompaniments of sex, and its evident unawareness that regular lovemaking is one of the things people get married for. He talks about married sex—the old friendly-affectionate, once-or-twice-a-week, hair-curlers-and-pajamas married sex that is the butt of a thousand jokes as old as the pyramids—as if it were a complicated and bizarre exercise in embarrassment.

It may not seem fair to tar a whole movement with the brush of Ramon, who could well be a bit touched in the head. But what about those faked statistics in the brochures he hands out? Those are not the product of Veronica Lueken's cult; they are right-to-life standard issue, printed and reprinted by the hundreds of thousands. It is hard to believe that pro-lifers who are saner and better educated than Ramon have never seen them. Why has there been no principled rejection of such tactics from the intellectuals of the movement—Cardinal O'Connor, Nat Hentoff, Feminists for Life? It has to mean something that the antiabortion movement would stoop to medical falsehoods, and what it means, I think, beyond a cynical willingness to bamboozle the young, is that deep down inside the antiabortionists know that there is no argument against a wanted abortion that isn't also an argument against a woman's right to consult her own well-being. If it were honorable, the pro-life movement would admit this.

It would acknowledge that legal abortion is a remarkably safe procedure—a woman is seven times more likely to die in childbirth—that millions of American women have undergone without impairing their bodies, fertility, minds or relation-ships. It would also acknowledge that an unwanted pregnancy carried to term sets a woman up—not invariably, of course, but often enough—for a very difficult life. It would make a straightforward argument that a pregnant woman has a moral duty to bear the child, no matter what negative consequences ensue. That argument, however, would win about as many adherents among the pregnant as natural family planning does among the married. So the movement uses pseudoscience to make abortions appear not only wrong but dangerous.

All the same, I feel sorry for Ramon. He seems like yet another of New York's lost sheep. "More sins are committed here than anywhere else in the world," he says. "Except for California." I've seen Lueken's followers around town and they all seem to have the same pale, pinched, thwarted look, the men scruffy and baffled, the women prim and furious. They remind me of the damaged, semicoherent letter-writers in

Nathanael West's *Miss Lonelyhearts*. Although the right-to-life movement has seized the rhetoric of closeness and caring, and has rather successfully cast the pro-choice movement as hyperindividualistic and antisocial, it would be hard to imagine a more solitary young man than Ramon, who has broken with his family for reasons he did not wish to go into, gives every indication of having had few or no relationships with women, works a lonely job and even pickets abortion clinics all by himself. When I asked him if he wanted children, he immediately answered, "Oh sure," and then added a little sadly, "But God doesn't let you have everything you want."

None of this is to say that Ramon is harmless. It's one thing to walk past a picket line into a movie; it's another to be called a murderer as you go to the doctor. According to Janine, the clinic director, some patients have been tremendously upset by Ramon. One woman wept to the point of throwing up, but she didn't call off her operation. Janine points out that the clinic performs many gynecological services besides abortion, including birth control counseling and treatment of venereal disease; it also distributes sample contraceptives at no cost. Patients arriving for appointments naturally resent Ramon's assumptions about their purpose. In fact, one of the people who came closest to knocking Ramon to the ground was the husband of a woman being treated following the miscarriage of a much-wanted pregnancy.

Although Ramon is uncomfortable when asked personal questions, the invasiveness of his own behavior is lost on him. Someone who thinks he is saving lives can, of course, persuade himself to overlook just about anything, but there is something voyeuristic and creepy about the way he sizes women up, approaching this young, fertile, dark-skinned one, ignoring that middle-aged, menopausal, white one. There are many things I found repellent about Ramon, but what outraged me most was that he felt entitled to see women's bodies—my body, which, by the way, he did not consider pamphlet material when I walked by as a stranger—as reproductive objects, wombs on legs. As much as any construction worker noisily ogling women walking down the street, Ramon treats women's privates as public property. He could, after all, accost the men entering the building, too; some of them are surely on their way up to the clinic to meet wives or girlfriends who've arrived separately, and the rest could file the pro-life message away for the future. But he never does.

Ramon is barred by law from standing in front of the door and from entering the common space of the building or the clinic itself. According to Janine, he has done all of those things. He has also followed her down the street calling her a licensed killer. When I asked Janine why she had never had him arrested, she told me that she hoped Ramon, and the three or four other demonstrators who take turns on Saturdays, would eventually get discouraged and go away. What they want, she said, is an incident that will attract media attention, and more demonstrators. "Maybe I'm being cowardly, but I keep thinking that if we just keep very quiet they'll leave us alone." Janine regularly receives obscene telephone calls at home accusing her of being a "bitch murderer."

What about Ramon's First Amendment right to freedom of speech? "We're having our rights infringed on much more than he would be if he had to stand away from people entering the building," said Janine. "That our privacy is being invaded doesn't seem to count legally." One lawyer I spoke with pointed out that "fighting words"—inflammatory and abusive language, like "licensed killer" and "murderer"—were not protected by the Constitution (although the same words might be acceptable if written on a placard). It's a gray area, though, and in any case Janine would have to swear out a complaint, risking the right-to-life wrath she is trying to avoid.

Perhaps Ramon is consciously trying to provoke violence; perhaps, which seems more likely, he is simply provoking by nature. But to the clinic staff, his very presence is a potent reminder of the possibility of violence. Although he told me he abhorred the recent wave of clinic bombings in New York City, it has not gone unnoticed at the clinic that the morning before the nighttime bombing of the Eastern Women's Center in midtown Manhattan he was absent from his usual post and did not reappear for a week. Ramon told me he was picketing a clinic in Queens that week and always alternates between the two on the theory that "you can save a life in Queens just as easily as in Manhattan." He also volunteered, as a story in the funny-coincidence department, that this Queens clinic was the very one outside of which three sticks of dynamite were found on the morning he switched back to Manhattan.

Janine's clinic has received several bomb threats, and the staff conducts weekly drills to practice evacuating patients in case a threat is received during clinic hours. "Abortion is stressful enough without this adding to it," said Janine. "I check the flowerpots every morning when I come in. You know, I always thought New York would be the last safe place. But I was wrong."

In mid-November, about a week after this conversation took place, a woman entering the building for an abortion fended Ramon off by flailing at him with her purse. Just before Thanksgiving, Janine saw Ramon in the lobby and reminded him that he was violating the law. When she came down again a half hour later, he was still there. She summoned the police, and when he refused to leave the building, he was arrested, handcuffed and booked on charges of disorderly conduct. He returned a few days later. On December 5 he was arrested a second time, for harassing visitors to the building. He returned once more, then disappeared, according to Janine, the day before the bombing of Planned Parenthood's Manhattan office, on December 14.

Janine expects to go to court some time in February. Meanwhile, bomb threats against the clinic have increased. And soon after New Year's, Ramon took up his old station outside the building.

1987

Lorena's Army

I didn't watch much of Lorena Bobbitt's trial. I was too busy trying to locate the hordes of feminists who, according to the media, were calling her a heroine and touting penis removal as a revolutionary act. Where were these people? The standard line on feminism, after all, is that it has been roundly rejected by American women—except for the odd antiporn frump and, of course, the campus P.C. crowd—and the reason for its unpopularity is its grim view of heterosexuality, its hatred of men and its insistence on seeing women as victims of male lust and violence. Even women who *are* feminists take this view. Naomi Wolf, Katie Roiphe, Elizabeth Fox-Genovese, have all issued some variant of this diagnosis and come up with the same advice to the women's movement: Lighten up and rejoin the mainstream: Men are not, repeat not, the enemy. Betty Friedan has been saying this sort of thing for years.

Now, suddenly, not only does the media insist that the

country is teeming with feminists but it is precisely man-hating
and rage and victim justification that have rallied the hitherto
invisible troops. Even Katie Roiphe, who thinks date rape is
mostly imaginary and the oppression of women a thing of the
past, has noticed that lots of women are really mad at men,
and presented this remarkable finding on the Op-Ed page of
The New York Times, although she was unable to say what,
beyond some Caliban-like darkness of the feminine soul,
caused women to feel so aggrieved.

Well, let me be fair. The *Times* did manage to find a self-
identified feminist who thought Lorena was fabulous, one
Stephanie Morris, who in a letter called her "a symbol of
innovative resistance against gender oppression everywhere."
But Morris was writing from Sydney, Australia. I call that
reaching. Here in America, the feminists I've seen in print
have made rather judiciously framed points, deploring violence while contrasting the big fuss made over John Bobbitt's
penis with the business-as-usual reality of rape, wife abuse
and, for millions of girls around the world, clitoridectomy.
Indeed, while the Bobbitts were monopolizing the headlines,
assorted husbands and boyfriends were committing mayhem
on the inside pages, and Maynard Merwine, a history instruc-
tor at Lehigh County Community College, published a letter
in the *Times* defending female genital mutilation as "an affirmation of the value of woman in traditional society" and "a
joyous occasion" for the girls involved. Maybe Stephanie
Morris should drop by his office for a little chat.

As it happens, I know a number of women's movement
heavies—writers, academics, lawyers—and not one of them
had anything bloodcurdling to say about the Bobbitt case. "I
don't care." "It's all so gruesome I don't even want to read
about it." "Isn't she kind of borderline retarded?" One noted
feminist theorist wondered if juries were too eager to absolve
defendants of personal responsibility. It was like talking to

George Will. The closest anyone would come to defending Lorena was to suggest that while, mind you, not condoning *in any way* slicing a male even as despicable as John Bobbitt (universal agreement there), you could sort of . . . maybe . . . see how she might have flipped out. Being borderline retarded and all.

Surprised? I wasn't. In real life, most women who call themselves feminists are nice, liberal, middle-class professionals. By socialization, education, political conviction and gender pride, they take a dim view of violence and place great weight on self-control, work, talking through problems and acting, in general, like a grown-up. They believe in safe sex, joint custody, voting, psychotherapy. Far from glamorizing victimhood, they have a quasi-religious faith in female "agency," which they manage to discern in some rather unlikely places, like brothels and jails. These are the women the women's movement has helped the most, and who, if anyone, can glimpse just around the corner a world in which men and women are friends—or if that seems too utopian, equal competitors for tenure. None of them would put up with a clueless brute like John Wayne Bobbitt for two minutes.

No, it's those regular mainstream I'm-no-feminist-I-shave-my-legs women who show their support for Lorena by scissoring their fingers in the V for victory sign. Women who are still trapped in the lesser life that feminist women have in many ways escaped—female-ghetto jobs, too much housework, too little respect, too many men like John Bobbitt. "I think she planned it," an elementary-school teacher told me. So should she have been convicted? "NO!"

"How can they make him a celebrity after what he did to her?" said a housecleaner. "They should try him again!" "Men have been getting away with abusing women for centuries," said a makeup artist. "If she struck back, good. Oh Christ, if I keep thinking like this I'll never find a man."

The current attack on "victim feminism" is partly a class phenomenon, a kind of status anxiety. It represents the wish of educated female professionals to distance themselves from stereotypes of women as passive, dependent, helpless and irrational. From this point of view, women like Lorena, if not punished, taint all women. Thus, in the *New York Post*, Andrea Peyser deplored the acquittal as a defeat for feminism, which ought to stand for "strength and competence." In the *New York Daily News*, Amy Pagnozzi claimed the verdict "infantilizes" women. Of course, by staking their gender's honor on individuals, feminists show that secretly they fear the stereotypes are true. You don't hear men complain that acquitting William Kennedy Smith infantilized all men.

Barbara Ehrenreich has suggested that the enthusiasm for Lorena among working-class, middle-American women shows that we need to think again about all those polls that show women supporting feminist issues but rejecting the feminist label. Maybe the troops are more militant than the generals.

If I were a man, I'd send NOW a check.

1994

Implants:
Truth and Consequences

The F.D.A. hearings into the safety of silicone gel breast implants have ended with a split recommendation by the advisory panel: Rejecting an outright ban on the devices, it urges that implantees be registered in clinical trials, to which only women who needed the surgery for reconstructive, not cosmetic, purposes would be guaranteed admittance. Which is it—"Panel Backs Marketing of Implants" (*The Washington Post*) or "Experts Suggest U.S. Sharply Limit Breast Implants" (*The New York Times*)? You be the judge.

Whatever else they were, the hearings were great theater. There was the perfidy of Dow (Napalm? Agent Orange? What's that?) Corning, the largest manufacturer of the implants, which was revealed to have lied and stonewalled for almost thirty years. There was the pious greed of plastic surgeons, who aggressively marketed the devices as a "cure" for "micromastia" (small breasts, to you) and now warn of an epidemic of "hysteria" in breast-enlarged women newly enlightened about the risks of autoimmune disorders, painful scarring, obscured mammograms. There was a hero, too, if a few decades late—David Kessler, the F.D.A.'s energetic new head. But most of all there were breasts—sex, beauty, fashion, women, women's bodies. Does anyone think the implant story would have been plastered all over the news media if it was about orthopedic shoes?

The real breast-implant story, though, isn't about women's bodies; it's about their minds. In the postfeminist wonderland in which we are constantly being told we live, women's lives are portrayed as one big smorgasbord of "choices" and "options," all value free and freely made, and which therefore cannot be challenged or even discussed, lest one sound patronizing or moralistic. Thus, women "choose" to have implants, we are told, to please men—no, wait, to boost their self-esteem—and who are you to criticize their judgment? But choice implies awareness of possible consequences, precisely what implantees were denied. And self-esteem does not occur in a vacuum but in response to social pressures and rewards. Isn't the question to ask, Why do so many women hate the breasts nature gave them so much? And why do they measure their self-esteem by the size of their bras? If breast augmentation really does increase their appeal to men—either directly or by making women feel more socially confident—and if being small-breasted really is a social disadvantage (which I must say I have not found it to be), how is implantation different from all the other awful things women have done to their bodies and their daughters' bodies in order to be marriageable? In premodern China a girl with natural-sized feet may well have felt unfeminine and embarrassed. In cultures that practice clitoridectomy, unmutilated girls are mocked by their sexually amputated peers. It's hard to feel much self-esteem when society tells you your body is deeply unacceptable. But shouldn't women be challenging the standards by which such judgments are made?

The language of options is seductive because it sounds so much like freedom and mutual respect. Even feminists fall for it: A few years back, *Ms.* ran a favorable article about Cher's total-body remake, and I seem to be the only person who thinks Jane Fonda's breast implants constitute false advertising both for her politics and her workout business. But the F.D.A. hearings show where the refusal to analyze the actual content of individual decisions ends up: in mutilated bodies and malpractice suits.

The next time medicine comes up with a cure for the "disease" of being female, let's let guinea pigs be the guinea pigs.

1992

The Smurfette Principle

This Christmas, I finally caved in: I gave my three-year-old daughter, Sophie, her very own cassette of *The Little Mermaid*. Now, she, too, can sit transfixed by Ariel, the perky teenager with the curvy tail who trades her voice for a pair of shapely legs and a shot at marriage to a prince. ("On land it's much preferred/for ladies not to say a word," sings the cynical sea witch, "and she who holds her tongue will get her man." Since she's the villain, we're not meant to notice that events prove her correct.)

Usually when parents give a child some item they find repugnant, they plead helplessness before a juvenile filibuster. But *The Little Mermaid* was my idea. Ariel may look a lot like Barbie, and her adventure may be limited to romance and over with the wedding bells, but unlike, say, Cinderella or Sleeping Beauty, she's active, brave and determined, the heroine of her own life. She even rescues the prince. And that makes her a rare fish, indeed, in the world of preschool culture.

Take a look at the kids' section of your local video store. You'll find that features starring boys, and usually aimed at them, account for nine out of ten offerings. Clicking the channel changer one recent week—admittedly not an encyclopedic study—I came across not a single network cartoon or puppet show starring a female. (Nickelodeon, the children's cable channel, has one of each.) Except for the crudity of the animation and the general air of witlessness and hype, I might as well have been back in my own 1950s childhood, nibbling Frosted Flakes in front of Daffy Duck, Bugs Bunny, Porky Pig and the rest of the all-male Warner Brothers lineup.

Contemporary shows are either essentially all-male, like "Garfield," or are organized on what I call the Smurfette principle: A group of male buddies will be accented by a lone female, stereotypically defined. In the worst cartoons— the ones that blend seamlessly into the animated cereal commercials—the female is usually a little-sister type, a bunny in a pink dress and hair ribbons who tags along with the adventurous bears and badgers. But the Smurfette principle rules the more carefully made shows, too. Thus, Kanga, the only female in "Winnie the Pooh," is a mother. Piggy, of "Muppet Babies," is a pint-size version of Miss Piggy, the camp glamour queen of the Muppet movies. April, of the wildly popular "Teen-Age Mutant Ninja Turtles," functions as a girl Friday to a quartet of male superheroes. The message is clear. Boys are the norm, girls are the variation; boys are central, girls peripheral; boys are individuals, girls types. Boys define the group, its story and its code of values. Girls exist only in relation to boys.

Well, commercial television—what did I expect? The surprise is that public television, for all its superior intelligence, charm and commitment to worthy values, shortchanges preschool girls, too. Mister Rogers lives in a neighborhood populated mostly by middle-aged men like himself. "Shining

Time Station" features a cartoon in which the male characters are train engines and the female characters are passenger cars. And then there's "Sesame Street." True, the human characters are neatly divided between the genders (and between the races, too, which is another rarity). The film clips, moreover, are just about the only place on television where preschoolers regularly see girls having fun together: practicing double Dutch, having a sleep-over. But the Muppets are the real stars of "Sesame Street," and the ones with real personalities, who sing on the musical videos, whom kids identify with and cherish in dozens of licensed products—are *all* male. I know one little girl who was so outraged and heartbroken when she realized that even Big Bird—her last hope—was a boy that she hasn't watched the show since.

Well, there's always the library. Some of the best children's books ever written have been about girls—Madeline, Frances the Badger. It's even possible to find stories with funny, feminist messages, like "The Paperbag Princess." (She rescues the prince from a dragon, but he's so ungrateful that she decides not to marry him, after all.) But books about girls are a subset in a field that includes a much larger subset of books about boys (twelve out of the fourteen storybooks singled out for praise in last year's Christmas roundup in *Newsweek*, for instance) and books in which the sex of the child is theoretically unimportant—in which case it usually "happens to be" male. Dr. Seuss's books are less about individual characters than about language and imaginative freedom—but, somehow or other, only boys get to go on beyond Zebra or see marvels on Mulberry Street. Frog and Toad, Lowly Worm, Lyle the Crocodile all *could* have been female. But they're not.

Do kids pick up on the sexism in children's culture? You bet. Preschoolers are like medieval philosophers: The text— a book, a movie, a TV show—is more authoritative than the evidence of their own eyes. "Let's play Wedding," says my

little niece. We grown-ups roll our eyes, but face it: It's still
the one scenario in which the girl is the central figure. "Women
are *nurses*," my friend Anna, a doctor, was informed by her
then-four-year-old, Molly. Even my Sophie is beginning to
notice the backseat role played by girls in some of her favorite
books. "Who's that?" she asks every time we re-read *The Cat
in the Hat*. It's Sally, the timid little sister of the resourceful
boy narrator. She wants Sally to matter, I think, and since
Sally is really just a name and a hair ribbon, we have to say
her name again and again.

The sexism in preschool culture deforms both boys and
girls. Little girls learn to split their consciousness, filtering
their dreams and ambitions through boy characters while ad-
miring the clothes of the princess. The more privileged and
daring can dream of becoming exceptional women in a man's
world—Smurfettes. The others are being taught to accept the
more usual fate, which is to be a passenger car drawn through
life by a masculine train engine. Boys, who are rarely confronted with stories in which males play only minor roles,
learn a simpler lesson: Girls just don't matter much.

How can it be that twenty-five years of feminist social
change have made so little impression on preschool culture?
Molly, now six and well aware that women can be doctors,
has one theory: Children's entertainment is mostly made by
men. That's true, as it happens, and I'm sure it explains a lot.
It's also true that, as a society, we don't seem to care much
what goes on with kids, as long as they are reasonably quiet.
Marshmallow cereal, junky toys, endless hours in front of the
tube—a society that accepts all that is not going to get in a
lather about a little gender stereotyping. It's easier to focus
on the bright side. I had *Cinderella*, Sophie has *The Little
Mermaid*—that's progress, isn't it?

"We're working on it," Dulcy Singer, the executive pro-
ducer of "Sesame Street," told me when I raised the sensitive

question of those all-male Muppets. After all, the show has only been on the air for a quarter of a century; these things take time. The trouble is, our preschoolers don't have time. My funny, clever, bold, adventurous daughter is forming her gender ideas right now. I do what I can to counteract the messages she gets from her entertainment, and so does her father—Sophie watches very little television. But I can see that we have our work cut out for us. It sure would help if the bunnies took off their hair ribbons, and if half of the monsters were fuzzy, blue—and female.

1991

Not Just Bad Sex

Stick to straight liquor," my father advised me when I left for college, in the fall of 1967. "That way, you'll always know how drunk you are." I thought he was telling me that real grown-ups didn't drink brandy Alexanders, but, of course, what he was talking about was sex. College boys could get totally plastered and the worst that would happen to them would be hangovers and missed morning classes. But if I didn't carefully monitor my alcohol intake one of those boys might, as they used to say, take advantage of me. Or, as they say now, date-rape me.

Veiled parental warnings like the one my father gave me —don't go alone to a boy's room, always carry "mad money" on a date, just in case—have gone the way of single-sex dorms, parietal hours, female-only curfews and the three-feet-on-the-floor rule, swept away like so much Victorian bric-a-brac by the sexual revolution, the student movement and the women's movement. The kids won; the duennas and fussbudgets lost.

Or did they? In *The Morning After: Sex, Fear, and Feminism on Campus* Katie Roiphe, a twenty-five-year-old Harvard alumna and graduate student of English at Princeton, argues that women's sexual freedom is being curtailed by a new set of hand-wringing fuddy-duddies: feminists. Antirape activists, she contends, have manipulated statistics to frighten college women with a nonexistent "epidemic" of rape, date rape and sexual harassment, and have encouraged them to view "everyday experience"—sexist jokes, professorial leers, men's straying hands and other body parts—as intolerable insults and assaults. "Stranger rape" (the intruder with a knife) is rare; true date rape (the frat boy with a fist) is even rarer. As Roiphe sees it, most students who say they have been date-raped are reinterpreting in the cold gray light of dawn the "bad sex" they were too passive to refuse and too enamored of victimhood to acknowledge as their own responsibility. Camille Paglia, move over.

These explosive charges have already made Roiphe a celebrity. The *Times Magazine* ran an excerpt from her book as a cover story: "Rape Hype Betrays Feminism." Four women's glossies ran respectful prepublication interviews; in *Mirabella* she was giddily questioned by her own mother, the writer Anne Roiphe. Clearly, Katie Roiphe's message is one that many people want to hear: Sexual violence is anomalous, not endemic to American society, and appearances to the contrary can be explained away as a kind of mass hysteria, fomented by man-hating fanatics.

How well does Roiphe support her case? *The Morning After* offers itself as personal testimony, with Roiphe—to use her own analogy—as a spunky, commonsensical Alice at the mad women's-studies-and-deconstructionism tea party familiar from the pages of Paglia and Dinesh D'Souza. As such, it's hard to challenge. Maybe Roiphe's classmates really are as she portrays them—waiflike anorexics, male-feminist wimps, the kind of leftist groupthinkers who ostracize anyone who says Alice Walker is a bad writer. Maybe Roiphe was, as she claims, "date-raped" many times and none the worse for it. The general tone of her observations is unpleasantly smug, but in her depiction of a tiny subculture on a few Ivy League campuses, she may well be onto something. The trouble is that *The Morning After*, although Roiphe denies this, goes beyond her own privileged experience to make general claims about rape and feminism on American campuses; it is also, although she denies this too, a "political polemic." In both respects, it is a careless and irresponsible performance, poorly argued and full of misrepresentations, slapdash research and gossip. She may be, as she implies, the rare grad student who has actually read *Clarissa*, but when it comes to rape and harassment she has not done her homework.

Have radical feminists inundated the nation's campuses with absurd and unfounded charges against men? Roiphe cites a few well-publicized incidents: at Princeton, for example, a student told a Take Back the Night rally that she had been date-raped by a young man she eventually admitted she had never met. But Roiphe's claim that such dubious accusations represent a new norm rests on hearsay and a few quotations from the wilder shores of feminist theory. "Recently," she writes, "at the University of Michigan, a female teaching assistant almost brought a male student up on charges of sexual harassment," because of some mildly sexist humor in a paper. When is "recently"? In what department of the vast University of Michigan did this incident occur? How does Roiphe know about it—after all, it only "almost" happened—and know that she got it right? Roiphe ridicules classmates for crediting and magnifying every rumor of petty sexism, but she does the

same: hysterical accusations are always being made at "a prominent university." Don't they teach the students at Harvard
and Princeton anything about research anymore?

Where I was able to follow up on Roiphe's sources, I found
some fairly misleading use of data. Roiphe accuses the legal
scholar Susan Estrich of slipping "her ideas about the nature
of sexual encounters into her legal analysis" in *Real Rape*, her
study of acquaintance rape and the law—one such idea supposedly being that women are so powerless that even "yes"
does not necessarily constitute consent to sex. In fact, in the
cited passage Estrich explicitly lays that view aside to pursue
her own subject, which is the legal system's victimization of
women who say *no*. Nowhere does Roiphe acknowledge
that—whatever may happen in the uncritical, emotional at-
mosphere of a Take Back the Night rally or a support-group
meeting for rape survivors (a term she mocks)—in the real
world women who have been raped face enormous obstacles
in obtaining justice in the courts or sympathy from their
friends and families. Nor does she seem to realize that it is
the humiliation and stigmatization and disbelief reported by
many rape victims, and documented in many studies, that
have helped to produce the campus climate of fear and cre-
dulity she deplores. Indeed, the only time Roiphe discusses
an actual court case it is to argue that the law veers too far to
the victim's side:

> In 1992 New Jersey's Supreme Court upheld its far-
> reaching rape laws. Ruling against a teenager charged with
> raping his date, the court concluded that signs of force or
> the threat of force is [*sic*] not necessary to prove the crime
> of rape—no force, that is, beyond that required for the phys-
> ical act of penetration. Both the plaintiff and the defendant
> admitted that they were sexually involved, but the two sides
> differed on whether what happened that night was rape. It's
> hard to define anything that happens in that strange, libid-

inous province of adolescence, but this court upheld the
judgment that the girl was raped. If the defendant had been
an adult he could have gone to jail for up to ten years. Susan
Herman, deputy public defender in the case, remarked,
"You not only have to bring a condom on a date, you have
to bring a consent form as well."

Roiphe should know better than to rely on a short item in
The Trenton Times for an accurate account of a complicated
court case, and she misrepresents even the sketchy information
the article contains: The girl was not the boy's "date," and
they did not both "admit" they were "sexually involved." The
two, indeed, disagreed about the central facts of the case. The
article does mention something Roiphe chose to omit: The girl
was fifteen years old. The Supreme Court opinion further
distinguishes this case from Roiphe's general portrait of date-
rape cases: the hypersensitive female charging an innocently
blundering male with a terrible crime for doing what came
naturally and doing it without a peep from her. The offender,
it turns out, was dating another girl living in the house where
the rape took place, and not the victim, who, far from passively
enduring his assault, did what Roiphe implies she did not:
She slapped him, demanded that he withdraw, and, in the
morning, told her mother, whereupon they went immediately
to the police. It is absurd to use this fifteen-year-old victim—
who had surely never heard of Catharine MacKinnon or Take
Back the Night—as an example of campus feminism gone
mad. And it is equally absurd to suggest that the highly regarded New Jersey Supreme Court, which consists of one
woman and six middle-aged men, issued a unanimous decision
in the victim's favor because it had been corrupted by radical
feminism.

The court did affirm that "signs of force or the threat of
force"—wounds, torn clothes, the presence of a weapon—

were not necessary to prove rape. This affirmation accords
with the real-life fact that the amount of force necessary to
achieve penetration is not much. But it is not true that the
court opened the door to rape convictions in the kinds of cases
Roiphe takes for the date-rape norm: sex in which the woman
says yes but means no, or says yes, means yes, but regrets it
later. The court said that consent, which need not be verbal,
must be obtained for intercourse. It's easy to parody this view,
as the defense counsel did with her joke about a "consent
form"—but all that it really means is that a man cannot pen-
etrate a woman without some kind of go-ahead. Roiphe ridicules this notion as "politically correct" and objects to
educational materials that remind men that "hearing a clear
sober 'yes' to the question 'Do you want to make love?' is very
different from thinking, 'Well, she didn't say no.' " But is that
such terrible advice? Roiphe herself says she wants women to
be more vocal about sex, yet here she is dismissive of the
suggestion that men ought to listen to them.

Roiphe's attempt to debunk statistics on the frequency of
rape is similarly ill-informed. A substantial body of research,
by no means all of it conducted by feminists, or even by
women, supports the contention that there is a staggering
amount of rape and attempted rape in the United States, and
that most incidents are not reported to the police—especially
when, as is usually the case, victim and offender know each
other. For example, the National Women's Study, conducted
by the Crime Victims Research and Treatment Center at the
Medical University of South Carolina, working under a grant
from the National Institute of Drug Abuse, which released
its results last year, found that 13 percent of adult American
women—one in eight—have been raped at least once, 75 percent by someone they knew. (The study used the conservative
legal definition of rape which Roiphe favors: "an event that
occurred without the woman's consent, involved the use of

force or threat of force, and involved sexual penetration of the victim's vagina, mouth or rectum.") Other researchers come up with similar numbers or even higher ones, and are supported by studies querying men about their own behavior: In one such study, 15 percent of the college men sampled said they had used force at least once to obtain intercourse.

Roiphe does not even acknowledge the existence of this sizable body of work—and it seems she hasn't spent much time studying the scholarly journals in which it appears. Instead, she concentrates on a single 1985 article in *Ms.* magazine, which presented a preliminary journalistic account of an acquaintance-rape study conducted by Dr. Mary Koss, a clinical psychologist now at the University of Arizona. Relying on opinion pieces by Neil Gilbert, a professor of social welfare at Berkeley, Roiphe accuses Koss of inflating her findings— one in eight students raped, one in four the victims of rape or attempted rape—by including as victims women who did not describe their experience as rape, although it met a widely accepted legal definition. It is unclear what Roiphe's point is —that women don't mind being physically forced to have sex as long as no one tells them it's rape? Surely she would not argue that the victims of other injustices—fraud, malpractice, job discrimination—have suffered no wrong as long as they are unaware of the law. Roiphe also accuses Koss of upping her numbers by asking respondents if they had ever had sex when they didn't want to because a man gave them alcohol or drugs. "Why aren't college women responsible for their own intake of alcohol or drugs?" Roiphe asks, and it may be fair to say that the alcohol question in the study is ambiguously worded. But it's worth noting that the question doesn't come out of feminist fantasyland. It's keyed to a legal definition of rape which in many states includes sex obtained by intentional incapacitation of the victim with intoxicants—the scenario envisioned by my father. Be that as it may, what happens to

Koss's figures if the alcohol question is dropped? The number of college women who have been victims of rape or attempted rape drops from one in four to one in five.

One in five, one in eight—what if it's "only" one in ten or twelve? Social science isn't physics. Exact numbers are important, and elusive, but surely what is significant here is that lots of different studies, with different agendas, sample populations and methods, tend in the same direction. Rather than grapple with these inconvenient data, Roiphe retreats to her own impressions: "If I was really standing in the middle of an epidemic, a crisis, if 25 per cent of my female friends were really being raped, wouldn't I know about it?" (Roiphe forgets that the one-in-four figure includes attempts, but let that pass.) As an experiment, I applied Roiphe's anecdotal method to myself, and wrote down what I knew about my own circle of acquaintance: eight rapes by strangers (including one on a college campus), two sexual assaults (one Central Park, one Prospect Park), one abduction (woman walking down street forced into car full of men), one date rape involving a Mickey Finn, which resulted in pregnancy and abortion, and two stalkings (one ex-lover, one deranged fan); plus one brutal beating by a boyfriend, three incidents of childhood incest (none involving therapist-aided "recovered memories"), and one bizarre incident in which a friend went to a man's apartment after meeting him at a party and was forced by him to spend the night under the shower, naked, while he debated whether to kill her, rape her or let her go. The most interesting thing about this tally, however, is that when I mentioned it to a friend he was astonished—he himself knew of only one rape victim in his circle, he said—but he knows several of the women on my list.

It may be that Roiphe's friends have nothing to tell her. Or it may be that they have nothing to tell *her*. With her adolescent certainty that bad things don't happen, or that they happen only to weaklings, she is not likely to be on the receiving end of many painful, intimate confessions. The one time a fellow-student tells her about being raped (at knifepoint, so it counts), Roiphe cringes like a high-school vegetarian dissecting her first frog: "I was startled. . . . I felt terrible for her. I felt like there was nothing I could say." Confronted with someone whose testimony she can't dismiss or satirize, Roiphe goes blank.

Roiphe is right to point out that cultural attitudes toward rape, harassment, coercion and consent are slowly shifting. It is certainly true that many women today, most of whom would not describe themselves as feminists, feel outraged by male behavior that previous generations—or even those women themselves not so long ago—quietly accepted as "everyday experience." Roiphe may even be right to argue that it muddies the waters when women colloquially speak of "rape" in referring to sex that is caddish or is obtained through verbal or emotional pressure or manipulation, or when they label as "harassment" the occasional leer or off-color comment. But if we lay these terms aside we still have to account for the phenomenon they point to: that women in great numbers—by no means all on elite campuses, by no means all young—feel angry at and exploited by behavior that many men assume is within bounds and no big deal. Like many of those men, Roiphe would like to short-circuit this larger discussion, as if everything that doesn't meet the legal definition of crime were trivial, and any objection to it mere paranoia. For her, sex is basically a boys' game, with boys' rules, like football, and if a girl wants to make the team—whether by "embracing experience" in bed or by attending a formerly all-male college —she has to play along and risk taking some knocks. But why can't women change the game, and add a few rules of their own? What's so "utopian" about expecting men to act as though there are two people in bed and two sexes in the classroom and the workplace?

Roiphe gives no consistent answer to this question. Sometimes she dismisses the problems as inconsequential: coerced intercourse is bad sex, widespread sexual violence a myth. Sometimes she suggests that the problem is real, but is women's fault: They should be more feisty and vociferous, be more like her and her friends, one of whom she praises for dumping a glass of milk on a boy who grabbed her breast. (Here, in a typical muddle, Roiphe's endorsement of assertive behavior echoes the advice of the antirape educational materials she excoriates.) Sometimes she argues that the women's movement has been so successful in moving women into the professions that today's feminists are whining about nothing. And sometimes she argues that men, if seriously challenged to change their ways and habits, will respond with a backlash, keeping women students at arm's length out of a fear of lawsuits, retreating into anxious nerdhood, like her male-feminist classmates, or even, like the male protagonist of David Mamet's *Oleanna*, becoming violent: "Feminists, Mamet warns, will conjure up the sexist beast if they push far enough."

Coming from a self-proclaimed bad girl and sexual rebel, this last bit of counsel is particularly fainthearted: Now who's warning women about the dangers of provoking the savage male? When Roiphe posits a split between her mother's generation of feminists—women eager to enter the world and seize sexual freedom—and those of today, who emphasize the difficulties of doing either, she has it wrong, and not just historically. (Sexual violence was a major theme of seventies feminism, in whose consciousness-raising sessions women first realized that rape was something many of them had in common.) The point she misses is that it was not the theories of academics or of would-be Victorian maidens masquerading as

Madonna fans that made sexual violence and harassment an issue. It was the movement of women into male-dominated venues—universities, professions, blue-collar trades—in sufficiently great numbers to demand real accommodation from men both at work and in private life. If Roiphe's contention that focusing on "victimhood" reduces women to passivity were right, the experience of Anita Hill would have sent feminists off weeping, en masse, to a separatist commune. Instead, it sparked a wave of activism that revitalized street-level feminism and swept unprecedented numbers of women into Congress.

Roiphe is so intent on demonizing the antirape movement that she misses an opportunity to address a real deficiency of much contemporary feminism. The problem isn't that acknowledging women's frequent victimization saps their get-up-and-go and allows them to be frail flowers; it's that the discourse about sexuality says so little about female pleasure. Unfortunately, Roiphe, too, is silent on this subject. We hear a lot about heavy drinking, late nights, parties, waking up in strange beds, but we don't hear what made those experiences worth having, except as acts of rebellion. In a revealing anecdote, she cites with approval a friend who tells off obscene phone callers by informing them that she was her high school's "blow job queen." Not to detract from that achievement, but one wonders at the unexamined equation of sexual service and sexual selfhood. Do campus bad girls still define their prowess by male orgasms rather than their own?

It's sad for Roiphe and her classmates that they are coming of age sexually at a time when sex seems more fraught with danger and anxiety than ever. Indeed, AIDS is the uneasily acknowledged spectre hovering over *The Morning After*: The condom, not the imaginary consent form, is what really put a damper on the campus sex scene. Certainly AIDS gives new urgency to the feminist campaign for female sexual self-determination, and has probably done a lot, at both conscious and unconscious levels, to frame that quest in negative rather than positive terms. But that's just the way we live now— and not only on campus. Rape, coercion, harassment, the man who edits his sexual history and thinks safe sex kills passion, the obscene phone call that is no longer amusing because you're not in the dorm anymore but living by yourself in a not-so-safe neighborhood and it's three in the morning: It's not very hard to understand why women sometimes sound rather grim about relations between the sexes.

It would be wonderful to hear more from women who are nonetheless "embracing experience," retaining the vital spark of sexual adventure. Roiphe prefers to stick to the oldest put-down of all: Problems? What problems? It's all in your head.

1993

Fetal Rights, Women's Wrongs

Some scenes from the way we live now:

In New York City, a pregnant woman orders a glass of wine with her restaurant meal. A stranger comes over to her table. "Don't you know you're poisoning your baby?" he says angrily, pointing to a city-mandated sign warning women that drinking during pregnancy can cause birth defects.

In California, Pamela Rae Stewart is advised by her obstetrician to stay off her feet, to eschew sex and "street drugs," and to go to the hospital immediately if she starts to bleed. She fails to follow this advice and delivers a brain-damaged baby who soon dies. She is charged with failing to deliver support to a child under an old criminal statute that was intended to force men to provide for women they have made pregnant.

In Washington, D.C., a hospital administrator asks a court whether it should intervene and perform a cesarean section on Angela Carder, seriously ill with cancer, against her wishes and those of her husband, her parents and her doctors. Acknowledging that the operation would probably shorten her life without necessarily saving the life of her twenty-five-week-old fetus, the judge nonetheless provides the order. The cesarean is performed immediately, before her lawyers can appeal. Angela Carder dies; so does her unviable fetus. That incident is subsequently dramatized on "L.A. Law," with postfeminist softy Ann Kelsey arguing for the hospital; on TV the baby lives.

In the Midwest, the U.S. Court of Appeals for the Seventh Circuit, ruling in *UAW* v. *Johnson Controls*, upholds an automotive battery plant's seven-year-old "fetal protection policy" barring fertile women (in effect, all women) from jobs that would expose them to lead. The court discounts testimony about the individual reproductive lives and plans of female employees (many in their late forties, celibate and/or with completed families), testimony showing that no child born to female employees had shown ill effects traceable to lead exposure and testimony showing that lead poses a comparable danger to male reproductive health. The court accepts testimony that says making the workplace safe would be too expensive.

All over the country, pregnant women who use illegal drugs and/or alcohol are targeted by the criminal justice system. They are "preventively detained" by judges who mete out jail sentences for minor crimes that would ordinarily result in probation or a fine; charged with child abuse or neglect (although by law the fetus is not a child) and threatened with manslaughter charges should they miscarry; and placed under court orders not to drink, although drinking is not a crime and does not invariably (or even usually) result in birth defects. While state legislatures ponder bills that would authorize these questionable practices by criminalizing drug use or "excessive" alcohol use during pregnancy, mothers are arrested in their hospital beds when their newborns test positive for drugs. Social workers increasingly remove positive-testing babies into foster care on the presumption that even a single use of drugs during pregnancy renders a mother ipso facto an unfit parent.

What's going on here? Right now the hot area in the developing issue of "fetal rights" is the use of drugs and alcohol during pregnancy. We've all seen the nightly news reports of inner-city intensive care units overflowing with crack babies, of Indian reservations where one in four children is said to be born physically and mentally stunted by fetal alcohol syndrome (F.A.S.) or the milder, but still serious, fetal alcohol effect. We've read the front-page stories reporting studies that suggest staggering rates of drug use during pregnancy (11 percent, according to *The New York Times*, or 375,000 women per year) and the dangers of even moderate drinking during pregnancy.

But drugs and alcohol are only the latest focus of a preoccupation with the fetus and its "rights" that has been wandering around the Zeitgeist for the past decade. A few years ago, the big issue was forced cesareans. (It was, in fact, largely thanks to the horrific Angela Carder case—one of the few involving a white, middle-class woman—that the American College of Obstetricians and Gynecologists condemned the practice, which nonetheless has not entirely ceased.) If the Supreme Court upholds the *Johnson Controls* decision, the next battleground may be the workplace. The "save the babies" mentality may look like a necessary, if troubling, approach when it's a matter of keeping a drug addict away from a substance that is, after all, illegal. What happens if the same mentality is applied to some fifteen to twenty million highly paid unionized jobs in heavy industry to "protect" fetuses that do not even exist? Or if the list of things women are put on legal notice to avoid expands to match medical findings on the dangers to the fetus posed by junk food, salt, aspirin, air travel and cigarettes?

Critics of the punitive approach to pregnant drug and alcohol users point out the ironies inherent in treating a public-health concern as a matter for the criminal justice system: the contradiction, for instance, of punishing addicted mothers-to-be when most drug treatment programs refuse to accept pregnant women. Indeed, Jennifer Johnson, a Florida woman who was the first person convicted after giving birth to a baby who tested positive for cocaine, had sought treatment and been turned away. (In her case the charge was delivering drugs to a minor.) The critics point out that threats of jail or the loss of their kids may drive women away from prenatal care and hospital deliveries, and that almost all the women affected so far have been poor and black or Latina, without private doctors to protect them. In Florida, nonwhite women are ten times as likely to be reported for substance abuse as white women, although rates of drug use are actually higher for whites.

These are all important points. But they leave unchallenged the notion of fetal rights itself. What we really ought to be asking is, How have we come to see women as the major threat to the health of their newborns, and the womb as the most dangerous place a child will ever inhabit? Why is our basic model "innocent" fetuses that would be fine if only presumably "guilty" women refrained from indulging their "whims"? The list of dangers to the fetus is, after all, very long; the list of dangers to children even longer. Why does maternal behavior, a relatively small piece of the total picture, seem such an urgent matter, while much more important factors—that one in five pregnant women receive no prenatal care at all, for instance—attract so little attention?

Here are some of the strands that make up the current tangle that is fetal rights:

The assault on the poor. It would be pleasant to report that the aura of crisis surrounding crack and F.A.S. babies—the urge to do *something*, however unconstitutional or cruel, that suddenly pervades society, from judge's bench to chic dinner party to six o'clock news—was part of a massive national campaign to help women have healthy, wanted pregnancies and healthy babies. But significantly, the current wave of concern is not occurring in that context. Judges order pregnant addicts to jail, but they don't order drug treatment programs to accept them, (many, citing insurance risks, refuse to accept pregnant women)—let alone order landlords not to evict them, or obstetricians to take uninsured women as patients, or the federal government to fully fund the Women, Infants, and Children supplemental feeding program, which reaches only two-thirds of those who are eligible. The policies that have underwritten maternal and infant health in most of the industrialized West since World War II—a national health service, paid maternity leave, direct payments to mothers, government-funded day care, home health visitors for new mothers, welfare payments that reflect the cost of living—are still regarded in the United States by even the most liberal as hopeless causes, and by everyone else as budget-breaking giveaways to the undeserving, pie-in-the-sky items from a mad socialist's wish list.

The focus on maternal behavior allows the government to appear to be concerned about babies without having to spend any money, change any priorities or challenge any vested interests. As with crime, as with poverty, a complicated, multifaceted problem is construed as a matter of freely chosen individual behavior. We have crime because we have lots of bad people, poverty because we have lots of lazy people (Republican version) or lots of pathological people (Democratic version), and tiny, sickly, impaired babies because we have lots of women who just don't give a damn.

Once the problem has been defined as original sin, coercion and punishment start to look like hardheaded and commonsensical answers. Thus, syndicated columnist and *New Republic* intellectual Charles Krauthammer proposes locking up pregnant drug users en masse. Never mind the impracticality of the notion—suddenly the same Administration that refuses to pay for drug treatment and prenatal care is supposed to finance all that plus nine months of detention for hundreds of thousands of women a year. Or its disregard of real life—what, for example, about the children those women already have? Do they go to jail, too, like the Dorrit children? Or join the rolls of the notorious foster care system? The satisfactions of the punitive mind-set sweep all such considerations aside. (Nor are liberal pundits immune from its spell. Around the same time Krauthammer was calling for mass incarceration, Mary McGrory was suggesting that we stop wasting resources— *what* resources?—on addicted women and simply put their babies in orphanages.)

The new temperance. While rightly sounding the alarm about the health risks and social costs of drugs, alcohol and nicotine, the various "just say no" crusades have so upped the moral ante across the board that it is now difficult to distinguish between levels and kinds of substance use and abuse and even rather suspect to try. A joint on the weekend is the moral equivalent of a twenty-four-hour-a-day crack habit; wine with meals is next door to a daily quart of rotgut. The stigmatizing of addicts, casual users, alcoholics, social drinkers and smokers makes punitive measures against them palatable. It also helps us avoid uncomfortable questions about why we are having all these "substance abuse" epidemics in the first place. Finally, it lets us assume, not always correctly, that drugs and alcohol, all by themselves, cause harm during pregnancy, and ignore the role of malnutrition, violence, chaotic lives, serious maternal health problems and lack of medical care.

Science marches on. We know a lot more about fetal development than we did twenty years ago. But how much of what we know will we continue to know in ten years? As recently as the early 1970s, pregnant women were harassed by their doctors to keep their weight down. They were urged to take tranquilizers and other prescription drugs, to drink in moderation (liquor was routinely used to stop premature labor), to deliver under anesthesia and not bother to breast-feed. Then, too, studies examined contemporary wisdom and found it good. Today, those precepts seem the obvious expression of social forces: the wish of doctors to control pregnancy and delivery, a lack of respect for women and a distaste for female physiological processes. It was not the disinterested progress of science that outmoded these practices. It was another set of social forces: the women's movement, the prepared-childbirth movement and the natural-health movement.

What about today's precepts? At the very least, the history of scientific research into pregnancy and childbirth ought to make us skeptical. Instead, we leap to embrace tentative findings and outright bad science because they fit current social prejudices. Those who argue for total abstinence during pregnancy have made much, for example, of a recent study in *The New England Journal of Medicine* that claimed women are more vulnerable than men to alcohol because they have less of a stomach enzyme that neutralizes it before it enters the bloodstream. Universally unreported, however, was the fact that the study included alcoholics and patients with gastrointestinal disease. It is a basic rule of medical research that results cannot be generalized from the sick to the healthy.

In a 1989 article in *The Lancet*, "Bias Against the Null Hypothesis: The Reproductive Hazards of Cocaine," Canadian researchers reported that studies that found a connection between cocaine use and poor pregnancy outcome had a better than even chance of being accepted for presentation at the annual meeting of the Society for Pediatric Research, while studies that found no connection had a negligible chance—although the latter were better designed. While it's hard to imagine that anyone will ever show that heavy drug use or alcohol consumption is good for fetal development, studies like this one suggest that when the dust settles (because the drug war is officially "won"? because someone finally looks at the newborns of Italy, where everyone drinks moderate amounts of wine with food, and finds them to be perfectly fine?) the current scientific wisdom will look alarmist.

Media bias. The assumptions that shape the way researchers frame their studies and the questions they choose to investigate are magnified by bias in the news media. Studies that show the bad effects of maternal behavior make the headlines, studies that show no bad effects don't get reported and studies that show the bad effects of paternal behavior (alcoholic males, and males who drink at conception, have been linked to lower I.Q. and a propensity to alcoholism in offspring) get two paragraphs in the science section. So did the study, briefly mentioned in a recent issue of *The New York Times*, suggesting that housewives run a higher risk than working women of having premature babies, stillbirths, underweight babies and babies who die in the first week of life. Imagine the publicity had it come out the other way around! Numbers that back up the feeling of crisis (those 375,000 drug-taking pregnant women) are presented as monolithic, although they cover a wide range of behavior (from daily use of cocaine to marijuana use during delivery, which some midwives recommend, and for which one Long Island woman lost custody of her newborn for eight months), and are illustrated by dire examples of harm that properly apply only to the most hard-core cases.

The "pro-life" movement. Antichoicers have not succeeded in criminalizing abortion but they have made it inaccessible to millions of women (only sixteen states pay for poor women's abortions, and only 18 percent of counties have even one abortion provider) and made it a badge of sin and failure for millions more. In Sweden, where heavy drinking is common, relatively few F.A.S. babies are born, because alcoholic women have ready access to abortion and it is not a stigmatized choice. In America antichoice sentiment makes it impossible to suggest to a homeless, malnourished, venereally diseased crack addict that her first priority ought to be getting well: Get help, then have a baby. While the possibility of coerced abortions is something to be wary of, the current policy of regulation and punishment in the name of the fetus ironically risks the same end. Faced with criminal charges, pregnant women may seek abortions in order to stay out of jail (a Washington, D.C., woman who "miscarried" a few days before sentencing may have done just that).

As lobbyists, antichoicers have sought to bolster their cause by interjecting the fetus-as-person argument into a wide variety of situations that would seem to have nothing to do with abortion. They have fought to exclude pregnant women from proposed legislation recognizing the validity of "living wills" that reject the use of life support systems (coma baby lives!), and have campaigned to classify as homicides assaults on pregnant women that result in fetal death or miscarriage. Arcane as such proposals may seem, they have the effect of broadening little by little the areas of the law in which the fetus is regarded as a person, and in which the woman is regarded as its container.

At a deeper level, the "pro-life" movement has polluted the way we think about pregnancy. It has promoted a model of pregnancy as a condition that by its very nature pits women and fetuses against each other, with the fetus invariably taking precedence, and a model of women as selfish, confused, potentially violent and incapable of making responsible choices. As the "rights" of the fetus grow and respect for the capacities and rights of women declines, it becomes harder and harder to explain why drug addiction is a crime if it produces an addicted baby, but not if it produces a miscarriage, and why a woman can choose abortion but not vodka. And that is just what the "pro-lifers" want.

The privileged status of the fetus. Pro-choice activists rightly argue that antiabortion and fetal-rights advocates grant fetuses more rights than women. A point less often made is that they grant fetuses more rights than two-year-olds—the right, for example, to a safe, healthy place to live. No court in this country would ever rule that a parent must undergo a medical procedure in order to benefit a child, even if that procedure is as riskless as a blood donation and the child is sure to die without it. (A Seattle woman is currently suing the father of her leukemic child to force him to donate bone marrow, but she is sure to lose, and her mere attempt roused *Newsday* science writer B. D. Colen to heights of choler unusual even for him.) Nor would a court force someone who had promised to donate a kidney and then changed his mind to keep his date with the organ bank. Yet, as the forced-cesarean issue shows, many of us seem willing to deny the basic right of bodily integrity to pregnant women and to give the fetus rights we deny children.

Although concern for the fetus may look like a way of helping children, it is actually, in a funny way, a substitute for it. It is an illusion to think that by "protecting" the fetus from its mother's behavior we have insured a healthy birth, a healthy infancy or a healthy childhood, and that the only insurmountable obstacle for crack babies is prenatal exposure to crack.

It is no coincidence that we are obsessed with pregnant women's behavior at the same time that children's health is declining, by virtually any yardstick one chooses. Take general well-being: In constant dollars, welfare payments are now about two-thirds the 1965 level. Take housing: Thousands of children are now growing up in homeless shelters and welfare hotels. Even desperately alcoholic women bear healthy babies two-thirds of the time. Will two-thirds of today's homeless kids emerge unscathed from their dangerous and lead-permeated environments? Take access to medical care: Inner-city hospitals are closing all over the country, millions of kids have no health insurance and most doctors refuse uninsured or Medicaid patients. Even immunization rates are down: Whooping cough and measles are on the rise.

The "duty of care." Not everyone who favors legal intervention to protect the fetus is antichoice. Some pro-choicers support the coercion and punishment of addicts and alcoholics—uneasily, like some of my liberal women friends, or gleefully, like Alan Dershowitz, who dismisses as absurd the "slippery slope" argument (crack today, cigarettes tomorrow) he finds so persuasive when applied to First Amendment issues. For some years now bioethicists have been fascinated by the doctrine of "duty of care," expounded most rigorously by Margery Shaw and John Robertson. In this view, a woman can abort, but once she has decided to bear a child she has a moral, and should have a legal, responsibility to insure a healthy birth. It's an attractive notion because it seems to combine an acceptance of abortion with intuitive feelings shared by just about everyone, including this writer, that pregnancy is a serious undertaking, that society has an interest in the health of babies, that the fetus, although not a person, is also not property.

Whatever its merits as a sentiment, though, the duty of care is a legal disaster. Exactly when, for instance, does the decision to keep a pregnancy take place? For the most desperately addicted—the crack addicts who live on the subway or prostitute themselves for drugs—one may ask if they ever form any idea ordinary people would call a decision, or indeed know they are pregnant until they are practically in labor. Certainly the inaccessibility of abortion denies millions of women the ability to decide.

But for almost all women the decision to carry a pregnancy to term has important, if usually unstated, qualifications. What one owes the fetus is balanced against other considerations, such as serious health risks to oneself (taking chemotherapy or other crucial medication), or the need to feed one's family (keeping a job that may pose risks) or to care for the children one already has (not getting the bed rest the doctor says you require). Why should pregnant women be barred from considering their own needs? It is, after all, what parents do all the time. The model of women's relation to the fetus proposed by the duty-of-care ethicists is an abstraction that ignores the realities of life even when they affect the fetus itself. In real life, for instance, to quit one's dangerous job means to lose one's health insurance, thus exposing the fetus to another set of risks.

It is also, even as an abstraction, a false picture. Try as she might, a woman cannot insure a healthy newborn; nor can statistical studies of probability (even well-designed ones) be related in an airtight way to individual cases. We know that cigarettes cause lung cancer, but try proving in a court of law that cigarettes and not air pollution, your job, your genes or causes unknown caused *your* lung cancer.

Yet far from shrinking from the slippery slope, duty-of-care theorists positively hurl themselves down it. Margery Shaw, for instance, believes that the production of an imperfect newborn should make a woman liable to criminal charges and "wrongful life" suits if she knows, or should have known, the risk involved in her behavior, whether it's drinking when her period is late (she has a duty to keep track of her cycle), delivering at home when her doctor advises her not to (what doctor doesn't?) or failing to abort a genetically damaged fetus (which she has a duty to find out about). So much for that "decision" to bear a child—a woman can't qualify it in her own interests but the state can revoke it for her on eugenic grounds.

As these examples show, there is no way to limit the duty of care to cases of flagrant or illegal misbehavior—duty is duty, and risk is risk. Thus, there is no way to enshrine the duty of care in law without creating the sort of Romania-style fetal-police state whose possibility Dershowitz, among others, pooh-poohs. For there is no way to define the limits of what a pregnant woman must sacrifice for fetal benefit, or what she "should have known," or at what point a trivial risk becomes significant. My aunt advised me to get rid of my cats while I was pregnant because of the risk of toxoplasmosis. My doctor and I thought this rather extreme, and my husband simply took charge of the litter box. What if my doctor had backed up my aunt instead of me? If the worst had happened (and it always does to someone, somewhere), would I have been charged with the crime of not sending my cats to the Bide-A-Wee?

Although duty-of-care theorists would impose upon women a virtually limitless obligation to put the fetus first, they impose that responsibility *only* on women. Philosophy being what it is, perhaps it should not surprise us that they place no corresponding duty upon society as a whole. But what about Dad? It's his baby, too, after all. His drug and alcohol use, his prescription medications, his workplace exposure and general habits of health not only play a part in determining the quality of his sperm but affect the course of pregnancy as well. Cocaine dust and smoke from crack, marijuana and tobacco present dangers to others who breathe them; his addictions often bolster hers. Does he have a duty of care to make it possible for his pregnant partner to obey those judge's orders and that doctor's advice that now has the force of law? To quit his job to mind the children so that she can get the bed rest without which her fetus may be harmed? Apparently not.

The sexist bias of duty of care has already had alarming legal consequences. In the Pamela Rae Stewart case cited at the beginning of this article, Stewart's husband, who had heard the doctor's advice, ignored it and beat his wife into the bargain. Everything she did, he did—they had sex together, smoked pot together, delayed getting to the hospital together—but he was not charged with a crime, not even with wife-beating, although no one can say that his assaults were not a contributing cause of the infant's injury and death. In Tennessee, a husband succeeded in getting a court order forbidding his wife to drink or take drugs, although he himself had lost his driver's license for driving while intoxicated. In Wyoming, a pregnant woman was arrested for drinking when she presented herself at the hospital for treatment of injuries inflicted by her husband. Those charges were dropped (to be reinstated, should her baby be born with defects), but none were instituted against her spouse.

It is interesting to note in this regard that approximately one in twelve women is beaten during pregnancy, a time when many previously nonviolent men become brutal. We do not know how many miscarriages, stillbirths and damaged newborns are due, or partly due, to male violence—this is itself a comment on the skewed nature of supposedly objective scientific research. But if it ever does come to be an officially recognized factor in fetal health, the duty of care would probably take yet another ironic twist and hold battered pregnant women liable for their partner's assaults.

The Broken Cord, Michael Dorris's much-praised memoir of his adopted F.A.S. child, Adam, is a textbook example of the way in which all these social trends come together—and the largely uncritical attention the book has received shows how seductive a pattern they make. Dorris has nothing but contempt for Adam's birth mother. Perhaps it is asking too much of human nature to expect him to feel much sympathy for her. He has witnessed, in the most intimate and heartbreaking way, the damage her alcoholism did, and seen the ruin of his every hope for Adam, who is deeply retarded. But why is his anger directed only at her? Here was a seriously alcoholic woman, living on an Indian reservation where heavy drinking is a way of life, along with poverty, squalor, violence, despair and powerlessness, where, one might even say, a kind of racial suicide is taking place, with liquor as the weapon of choice. Adam's mother, in fact, died two years after his birth from drinking antifreeze.

Dorris dismisses any consideration of these facts as bleeding-heart fuzzy-mindedness. Like Hope on "thirtysomething," Adam's mother "decides" to have a baby; like the martini-sipping pregnant woman he badgers in an airport bar, she "chooses" to drink out of "weakness" and "self-indulgence."

Dorris proposes preventive detention of alcoholic pregnant women and quotes sympathetically a social worker who thinks the real answer is sterilization. Why do alcoholic Indian women have so many children? To up their government checks. (In fact, Bureau of Indian Affairs hospitals are prohibited by law from performing abortions, even if women can pay for them.) And why, according to Dorris, do they drink so much in the first place? Because of the feminist movement, which has undermined the traditional temperance of reservation women.

The women's movement has had about as much effect on impoverished reservation dwellers as it had on the slum-dwelling women of eighteenth-century London, whose heavy binge drinking—and stunted babies—appalled contemporary observers. That Dorris pins the blame on such an improbable villain points to what fetal rights is really about—controlling women. It's a reaction to legalized abortion and contraception, which has given women, for the first time in history, real reproductive power. They can have a baby, they can "kill" a baby, they can refuse to conceive at all, without asking permission from anyone. More broadly, it's an index of deep discomfort with the notion of women as self-directed social beings, for whom parenthood is only one aspect of life, as it has always been for men. Never mind that in the real world, women still want children, have children and take care of children, often under the most discouraging circumstances and at tremendous emotional, economic and physical cost. There is still a vague but powerful cultural fear that one of these days, women will just walk out on the whole business of motherhood and the large helpings of humble pie we, as a society, serve along with it. And *then* where will we be?

Looked at in this light, the inconsistent and fitful nature of our concern about the health of babies forms a pattern. The threat to newborns is interesting when and only when it can, accurately or fancifully, be laid at women's doorstep. Babies "possibly" impaired by maternal drinking? Front-page stories, a national wave of alarm. But a *New England Journal of Medicine* report that 16 percent of American children have been mentally and neurologically damaged because of exposure to lead, mostly from flaking lead paint in substandard housing? Peter

Jennings looks mournful and suggests that "all parents can do" is to have their children tested frequently. If the mother isn't to blame, no one is to blame.

In its various aspects, the doctrine of "fetal rights" attacks virtually all the gains of the women's movement. Forced medical treatment attacks women's increased control over pregnancy and delivery by putting doctors back in the driver's seat, with judges to back them up. Workplace fetal-protection policies contest the entry of women into high-paying, unionized, traditionally male jobs. In the female ghetto, where women can hardly be dispensed with, the growing practice of laying off or shifting pregnant women around transforms women, whose rates of labor-force participation are approaching those of men, into casual laborers with reduced access to benefits, pensions, seniority and promotions. In a particularly vicious twist of the knife, "fetal rights" makes legal abortion—which makes all the other gains possible—the trigger for a loss of human rights. Like the divorce courts judges who tell middle-aged housewives to go out and get a job, or who favor the father in a custody dispute because to recognize the primary-caretaker role of the mother would be "sexist," protectors of the fetus enlist the rhetoric of feminism to punish women.

There are lots of things wrong with the concept of fetal rights. It posits a world in which women will be held accountable, on sketchy or no evidence, for birth defects; in which all fertile women will be treated as potentially pregnant all the time; in which courts, employers, social workers and doctors—not to mention nosy neighbors and vengeful male partners—will monitor women's behavior. It imposes responsibilities without giving women the wherewithal to fulfill them, and places upon women alone duties that belong to both parents and to the community.

But the worst thing about fetal rights is that it portrays a woman as having only contingent value. Her work, her health, her choices and needs and beliefs, can all be set aside in an instant because, next to child-bearing, they are all perceived as trivial. For the middle class, the idea of fetal rights is mostly symbolic, the gateway to a view of motherhood as self-sacrifice and endless guilty soul-searching. It ties in neatly with the currently fashionable suspicion of working mothers, day care and (now that wives are more likely than husbands to sue for it) divorce. For the poor, for whom it means jail and loss of custody, it becomes a way of saying that women can't even be mothers. They can only be potting soil.

The plight of addicted and alcohol-impaired babies is indeed a tragedy. Finally, we are forced to look at the results of our harsh neglect of the welfare and working poor, and it's only natural that we don't like what we see. We are indeed in danger of losing a generation. But what about the generation we already have? Why is it so hard for us to see that the tragedy of Adam Dorris is inextricable from the tragedy of his mother? Why is her loss—to society, to herself—so easy to dismiss?

"People are always talking about women's duties to others," said Lynn Paltrow, the A.C.L.U. lawyer who successfully led the Pamela Rae Stewart defense, "as though women were not the chief caregivers in this society. But no one talks about women's duty of care to *themselves*. A pregnant addict or alcoholic needs to get help for *herself*. She's not just potentially ruining someone else's life. She's ruining her own life.

"Why isn't her own life important? Why don't we care about her?"

1990

A NOTE ON THE TYPE

This book was set in Janson, a redrawing of type
cast from matrice long thought to have been made
by the Dutchman Anton Janson, who was a practicing typefounder in Leipzig during the years
1668–87. However, it has been conclusively demonstrated that these types are actually the work of
Nicholas Kis (1650–1702), a Hungarian, who most
probably learned his trade from the master Dutch
typefounder Dirk Voskens. The type is an excellent
example of the influential and sturdy Dutch types
that prevailed in England up to the time William
Caslon developed his own incomparable designs
from them.

Composed by PennSet, Inc.,
Bloomsburg, Pennsylvania

Printed and bound by
Arcata Graphics/Martinsburg
Martinsburg, West Virginia

Typography and binding design by
Dorothy Schmiderer Baker